PRAISE FOR *The Next Jihad*

"*The Next Jihad* is a vivid and timely primer on the religious terror now targeting Christians in large regions of the African country of Nigeria. That, for its faith, this church community—the largest Christian community of the most Christian continent today—suffers relentless, unspeakable death and torment at the hands of those who align with Islamic State and other extremists should at once inspire us and serve as a warning. Yet Rev. Johnnie Moore and Rabbi Abraham Cooper show that the courageous witness of these African Christians is met by silence as their own government and the international community respond with cold indifference. Read this compelling book and learn why we should act while there is still time."

—NINA SHEA, DIRECTOR, HUDSON INSTITUTE'S
CENTER FOR RELIGIOUS FREEDOM

"Rabbi Cooper and Johnnie Moore have written a compelling firsthand account of the unfolding tragedy in Nigeria, Africa's most populous nation. They write with clarity, insight, and urgency about an unfolding genocide, driven by Jihadist ideology and hatred of difference.

"They detail the hacking to death and beheading of Christians; the destruction of homes, livelihoods, and places of worship; and the abduction and rape of young women—personified by the story of Leah Sharibu—and they ask, why are we so indifferent?

"This book is a timely and overdue call to action—with fifteen concluding recommendations—reminding us that 'quiet diplomacy didn't save six million Jews,' that 'never again' is a glib slogan that has been rendered meaningless in Jos, Kano, Plateau State, and Nigeria's many other slaughterhouses.

"This is a powerful message that demands the attention of us all, and it ought to be on every leader's desk. We have voices, votes, freedoms, privileges—and having read this book, you will have no excuse for not using them."

—T

"Rabbi Abraham Cooper and Rev. Johnnie Moore have long been numbered among the world's foremost advocates for religious freedom and human rights. I'm very glad they have turned their attention to Nigeria, where there is an ongoing genocide largely ignored by the world. They have led by example by traveling there themselves before writing this well-researched and compelling call to action. The world must act now."

—REP. FRANK WOLF, US HOUSE OF REPRESENTATIVES (1981-2015)

THE NEXT JIHAD

The NEXT JIHAD

STOP THE CHRISTIAN GENOCIDE IN AFRICA

REV. JOHNNIE MOORE AND
RABBI ABRAHAM COOPER

W PUBLISHING GROUP

AN IMPRINT OF THOMAS NELSON

The Next Jihad
© 2020 Johnnie Moore and Rabbi Abraham Cooper

Published in Nashville, Tennessee, by W Publishing Group, an imprint of
Thomas Nelson.

Published in association with Yates & Yates, www.yates2.com.

Thomas Nelson titles may be purchased in bulk for educational, business,
fundraising, or sales promotional use. For information, please e-mail
SpecialMarkets@ThomasNelson.com.

Unless otherwise indicated, all Scripture quotations taken from The Holy
Bible, New International Version®, NIV®. © 1973, 1978, 1984, 2011 by Biblica,
Inc.® Used by permission of Zondervan. All rights reserved worldwide.

Scripture quotations marked ESV taken from The ESV® Bible (The Holy
Bible, English Standard Version®), © 2001 by Crossway, a publishing
ministry of Good News Publishers. Used by permission. All rights reserved.

The names and identifying details of some of the individuals discussed in
this book have been changed to protect their privacy.

Any internet addresses, phone numbers, or company or product information
printed in this book are offered as a resource and are not intended in any
way to be or to imply an endorsement by Thomas Nelson, nor does Thomas
Nelson vouch for the existence, content, or services of these sites, phone
numbers, companies, or products beyond the life of this book.

ISBN 978-0-7852-4147-8 (eBook)

Library of Congress Control Number: 2020942389

ISBN 978-0-7852-4134-8 (TP)

Printed in the United States of America

20 21 22 23 24   LSC   10 9 8 7 6 5 4 3 2 1

To the victims of terrorism and ethnic cleansing in Nigeria:
You are not forgotten.
We will not be silent.

It is not your responsibility to finish the work,
but you are not free to desist from it.

—ETHICS OF THE FATHERS 2:16

CONTENTS

A Note to the Reader

In addition to writing about the atrocities committed by Boko Haram and Islamic State (IS) in West Africa, we've also written at length about the atrocities committed by Fulani militants.

In this book, therefore, you will find occasional references to "Fulani *militants*." We have chosen this term over the more common "Fulani *tribesmen*" to distinguish between the actual militants and the scores of peace-loving Fulani tribespeople throughout Nigeria and the broader region. The tribespeople have nothing to do with the terrorism committed by some of their kinsmen and are often themselves victims of atrocities.

Also, it is not our intention to infer that people in the government in Nigeria who are Fulani Muslims themselves are necessarily affiliated, directly or indirectly, with the Fulani militants. Rather, we believe there are people of influence in the government who want to find a peaceful and prosperous future for all of the citizens of Nigeria, irrespective of their religion or ethnicity.

We anticipate being accused of politicizing religion by addressing its role in Nigeria's conflict, but we believe that religion isn't just at the heart of the crisis in Nigeria but also may be the key to the solution.

Finally, we have, in certain circumstances, changed the names or identifying characteristics of victims to protect their privacy.

Prologue

ON THE COLLABORATION OF A
REVEREND AND A RABBI

We're guessing this may be the first time you've read a book coauthored by an evangelical pastor and an orthodox Jewish rabbi.

Don't worry. You're not the only one.

There aren't very many books like this.

For centuries collaboration between Jewish and Christian clergy was challenging—and sometimes impossible. The enmity between our separate branches of Abraham's tree has been real. The truth is that *trust* was the last word to come to mind when reflecting on nearly two millennia of Christendom's theological and practical maltreatment of Jews. Christians, including over 75 percent of Hitler's Nazis, were often enablers or practitioners of the world's worst anti-Semitism. Jews have often struggled to trust the motives of Christian friendship when Christianity is so fixated on conversion.

As Rabbi Jonathan Sacks has reminded us, "None of the great

religions can say, in unflinching self-knowledge: 'Our hands never shed innocent blood.'"[1]

Yet the complexity of our history makes the unique friendship now shared between evangelicals and Jews among the great miracles of our modern era. In a world where anti-Semitism remains persistent and inundates governments, traditional media, the internet, and international organizations, it is often the millions of Christian friends of the Jewish people who multiply the voices of the world's sixteen million Jews and the State of Israel. Evangelical Christians, by the sheer size of their movement (now exceeding seven hundred million), may now stand as the world's primary bulwark against anti-Zionism, the current, most potent mutation of historical anti-Semitism.

Conversely, the moral voice of the Jewish people has been deployed again and again to defend persecuted Christians around the world, often before Christians themselves have spoken up. The Simon Wiesenthal Center was the first organization to state that ISIS' 2014 targeting of Christians in the Middle East represented genocide—months before any major Christian organization made such a declaration.

Today Christians and Jews—who each cling to their own theological beliefs—are increasingly bound together, especially in a shared love for Israel.

Collaboration on other fronts is still emerging. For instance, Christians generally have not discovered the volumes upon volumes of Jewish commentary on our shared Hebrew Bible (what Christians call the Old Testament and what Jews call the Torah and Tanach). And in today's polarized American politics, Jews and Christians tend to work separately on issues of mutual concern rather than collaborating.

This is where we come in.

Our passion, as Jewish and Christian clergy, is to advance human rights and to protect religious freedom around the world. While our friendship transcends our work, fighting in the trenches together has animated our relationship, and the underpinnings of this collaboration are facilitated by a shared love of our country, the United States of America.

We are from different generations, practice different religions, and even live on different sides of the nation. Yet our work together has taken us all around the world; we have recently traveled together to Asia, Africa, and the Middle East. In mixed settings we sometimes refer to each other as the other's "pastor" or "rabbi," to lots of laughter.

The Rabbi has advocated for human rights for over fifty years and on every continent, cutting his teeth behind the Iron Curtain as a fierce savior of Jews during the Soviet Jewry movement. He helped bring to justice Nazis hiding throughout Europe, the Americas, and Australia; he held Silicon Valley accountable for enabling hate online; and his words echo throughout the halls of global power when anyone treats anti-Semitism lightly or embraces any other form of injustice.

The Reverend is a millennial who has spent much of his life wandering from country to country helping those in need. He shot to international renown at the height of the crisis with ISIS in Iraq and Syria after traveling to the region and documenting the abuses of Christians and Yazidis in his book *Defying ISIS*.

Then he raised millions of dollars to resettle or evacuate the vulnerable people, prompting the Simon Wiesenthal Center to make him their youngest ever recipient of a Medal of Valor.

What unites us isn't only our commitment to human rights and religious freedom but also our commitment to be people of *action*.

Jewish sages wrote, calling our attention to an active life in pursuit of an active faith, that the world stands on three things: Torah [G-d's word], service, and acts of loving kindness.[2] You can't do any of those things without action. The Christian New Testament says "faith without deeds is dead" (James 2:26).

We are committed to *acting* not just *advocating* to save lives.

We are also committed to doing our work as a Jew and as a Christian, respectively. Both of our religious communities have sometimes been concerned that interfaith work requires diluting theology and tradition as a prerequisite for cooperation.

We don't embrace this premise.

We believe we can do the most good together by being exactly and distinctly who we are. We respect our differences, which is one reason this book will reference the Almighty in this way: G-d. In Judaism the reverence for the Almighty extends to the way his name is written. That reverence for G-d is probably something we all could use a little more of, Jewish or not.

In fact, we now use a different phrase to describe our personal collaboration. We call our approach *multifaith* as opposed to *interfaith*; we aren't aiming to become less Christian or less Jewish as we work hand in hand to address the abuse of humans around the world, or—to put it positively—to protect the unique dignity of every human being made in G-d's image. Our mission is to make sure they are treated as they deserve—as his image bearers—for "whoever is kind to the poor lends to the LORD" (Proverbs 19:17).

Another lesson we've both learned, though forty years apart in age, is that when you're trying to help people in desperate need, your most important responsibility is to amplify their voices—to be the voice of the voiceless. We've learned to show up, not just in acts of solidarity with the forgotten but in using our own voices to ensure that they are no longer forgotten.

With G-d's help, and the help of people of faith, we can speak for those who cannot speak for themselves and *together* change the course of the mighty river of fate. This commitment is what brings us to this book and is, perhaps, why a rabbi and a pastor would together write a book about Africa.

To be honest, we are the most surprised. We thought we'd first write a different book together, but there's an emergency on the great continent that demands action.

And we go where *action* is required.

Introduction

WHAT'S GOING ON IN AFRICA?

*A*frica is a continent that takes up much of our globe but so little of our minds here in the West. It's an incomparably important place to our planet, yet it too rarely captures the world's attention.

Normally it does so only during tragedy. One may think of the Ebola epidemic or the genocide in Rwanda. Both exhibited warning signs that were largely ignored by the world until the cost of human life became absolutely unbearable and its effects spilled into public policy in the West.

It shouldn't be this way.

We are admirers of the great continent, a place of intrigue and opportunity. It is filled with extraordinary history and stunning people, rich in resources and natural beauty. But Africa has also been a place of pillaging by colonial powers and corruption by postcolonial leaders.

Now its every weakness is being exploited by opportunistic

terrorists who have found refuge in its sprawling forests, deserts, and underdeveloped places.

In some cases these terrorists have been expelled from the Middle East and have found a home in Africa. Other extremist groups have originated on the continent itself, drawing inspiration and strategy from al-Qaeda and ISIS, or vice versa, while attempting to anchor their authority in the continent's history with Islam and historic grievances with Western powers. Every step of the way there have also been bold Muslims opposing the terrorists' efforts. They have become their victims too.

As the pandemic of 2020—or 9/11 before it—reminds us, borders cannot contain the spread of disease, whether that disease is a coronavirus or the virus of hate fostered by extremists in vacuums of power around the world.

You could say the lights are blinking red again, but this time the threat is different. It's disparate and deeply embedded in Africa's largest and most influential countries, especially in Africa's most populous and oil-saturated Nigeria—our primary area of focus.

The next mutation of global terrorism has been cooking in Africa for some time. It has been running wild across the great continent, killing the innocent at will and en masse while destabilizing already fragile places along the way.

In our work we haven't seen a more delicate situation with more potentially dire consequences than what is brewing in Nigeria today. It spells human catastrophe for the world if it isn't curtailed, not to mention the tragedy it has already brought to the thousands of victims, some of whose stories are chronicled in this book.

We're also concerned that this *next jihad* may not only jeopardize the security of all of western Africa but take much of the world with it, especially an already weakening Europe.

Furthermore, Nigeria has the largest Christian population in Africa. If nothing is done, Christians will not be the last victims, for no person of any faith (Christian, Muslim, Hindu, Jew, or no faith at all) will be spared the ravages of terrorists who believe that their profane mission of death is in service to G-d.

There's still time for us to act before this threat destroys its hosts and is further exported to the streets of Europe and Australia, India and the United States. And we mean all of us: faith leaders from all religions, human rights activists, non-governmental organizations (NGOs), charitable individuals, and—of course—governments within and outside Africa.

Action will require leadership and resolve. It may require suspending what's politically correct on a continent that is still deeply entrenched in the global system, and it will especially take American leadership in cooperation with African and European leaders. It will take holding the line against an expansionist China, whose generous investments in Africa have come with very serious strings attached.

We love Africa. In fact, we love it too much to let the world remain in denial about how dangerous a challenge it faces. But we also love America and the freedoms that make our nation so exceptional. If Americans in the twenty-first century default to apathy and silence, Africa won't be the only land that is endangered.

We remember Winston Churchill's solemn warning to those in his day who were apathetic, silent, or even acquiescent during the rise of Nazism:

> Each one hopes that if he feeds the crocodile enough, the crocodile will eat him last. All of them hope that the storm will pass before their turn comes to be devoured. But I fear greatly that the storm will not pass. It will rage and it will roar ever more loudly, ever more widely.[1]

Is it not time that the good people get together and do some roaring of our own? The clock is ticking; as one victim told us, "Yesterday was the best day to act."

one

THE PERPETRATORS

*We are not a cancer. . . . The disease is
unbelief. . . . [E]veryone knows democracy is
unbelief, and everyone knows the constitution
is unbelief, and everyone knows that there are
things Allah has forbidden in the Qur'an . . .
[things] that are going on in western schools.*
—ABUBAKAR SHEKAU

We never dwelled on it, but in the weeks leading up to
our scheduled departure, we were shaken every time
we learned of another brutal attack in Nigeria. The mostly unspoken question was, *Why are we doing this?* Every time we
were able to put a name and face on even one unknown victim,
we knew we had to go. But the scope of one attack that took
place just days before our arrival shook us up. Such brazen,
cold-blooded, calculated brutality—how to make sense of it all?

We would soon learn that full answers and easy solutions would prove elusive.

The attack happened near the city of Auno in Borno State, not far from its capital, Maiduguri, after the travelers had been refused passage at a military checkpoint.[1]

According to CNN, the military officers told them that they couldn't enter the city after 4:00 p.m., so they were faced with two terrible options: turn back and drive all night through a dangerous area or sleep in their cars outside the gates of the city until the next morning.

They opted for the latter because it seemed safer, but that decision would prove fatal. Terrorist gunmen speeding past on motorcycles began spraying gunfire at the civilian cars. They eventually set nearly twenty vehicles on fire, burning alive the trapped victims. Those they didn't kill they kidnapped. Among the innocents ruthlessly massacred was a beautiful nineteen-year-old student named Fatima Babagana. She was studying political science at the University of Maiduguri to pursue a childhood dream of becoming a journalist. Within earshot of a military checkpoint, she and her traveling companions were left in a terrorist's fishbowl.[2]

The governor of Borno told the local media that the federal government's soldiers responsible for guarding the checkpoint normally just abandon their positions after 5:00 p.m., leaving the entire area vulnerable to the terrorists.[3] This was at least the sixth attack on Auno in less than a year.

One observer tweeted, How do you lock the city gate, leaving innocent citizens to sleep on the Highway in a conflict zone, without providing adequate protection for them? What kind of a Country is this?[4]

Welcome to Nigeria.

BOKO HARAM SEEKS A HOLY WAR

The group that committed the massacre in Auno is technically called *Jama'atu Ahlis Sunna Lidda'awati Wal-Jihad*. It means "People Committed to the Propagation of the Prophet's Teachings and Jihad."

The rest of the world calls them by a common local reference: *Boko Haram*. It brings together two words, one in the local Hausa language and the other in Arabic, and together they mean "Western education is forbidden."[5]

The group was once an "isolated sect in Northern Nigeria [that] came to reach out to international jihadists in the al-Qaeda network [before] later switching their allegiance to [ISIS]."[6] Their armed insurgency began in Northern Nigeria as early as 2009, but today their influence is multinational, stretching from northeastern Nigerian territories to the broader Lake Chad region, including northern Cameroon, western Chad, and Niger.[7]

Boko Haram became active long before taking up arms; the group formed in the early 1990s in Maiduguri, which was a "ramshackle city of just over a million people, draped along an ancient shoreline of Lake Chad called the Bama Ridge."[8]

The name *Boko Haram* may initially seem strange for a terrorist organization, but it isn't when you understand a bit more about the history of Nigeria—a history in which Islam came and conquered before eventually settling into a delicate but uneasy balance with outside influences and European colonial powers. This was accompanied by growing conflict within Muslim leadership.

Scott MacEachern provides helpful context:

> The religious and political roots of Boko Haram extend much further back in time, however, to the coming of Islam to this part of Africa. People do not realize the long history of Islam and the African continent, especially between the Atlantic and Lake Chad in West Africa, and along the East African coast. . . . Muslims certainly lived . . . northeast of Lake Chad, by the early eleventh century . . . [and] rulers of Islamic states [in the region, then] made accommodations with the religions of their non-Muslim subjects. . . . By the seventeenth century, controversies concerning Islam began to bubble up across this part of the continent. Reformist [conservative] Muslim clerics criticized the reigning Muslim rulers for being both wicked in their governance and lax in their duties as Muslims and in their responsibility for converting their citizens to Islam. They replaced the earlier elite tolerance of non-Muslim practice with a purer, more rigorous and more inclusive form of Islam, one that encompassed the entire state within the *dar al-Islam*. . . . Muslim reformers put those critiques into action in a series of jihads.[9]

That West African expansion of Islam eventually led to the "Lake Chad Basin by the late eighteenth century, when a reformist Fulani cleric named Usman dan Fodio overthrew the Hausa rulers of Northern Nigeria . . . establishing the Sokoto Caliphate [which] lasted until the coming of European colonial powers a century later."[10]

Much criticism is levied against the vices of colonialists. But a Yale scholar from Gambia, the late Lamin Sanneh—whom we dined with in Los Angeles not long before his sudden passing in early 2019—helps us see that "colonial rule introduced modern, global forces—political and economic—into the Muslim world."[11] This resulted in a "judicious mix of policies . . . [that] enabled the Islamization of society rather than the Islamization of the state," which Sanneh argues "undercut [the preceding years of] armed jihad."[12]

Yet to solidify their control, the British rulers also cut a deal with the historic Islamic leaders and "promised the emirs [of Northern Nigeria] that there would be no interference in religious matters and interpreted this to mean that Islam would be upheld as the religion of any state whose ruler called himself a Muslim." As a result, the British, as Sanneh has noted, "enabled Islamic law to gain greater influence."[13]

Nigeria, then, has a long history, ancient and present, when it comes to the institution of Islamic law in various forms throughout its northern states. Some rejected and felt threatened by new values the nation adopted when it became a democracy, and in the 1990s some seized the moment to entrench Islamic law throughout the Muslim North.

Boko Haram emerged during this "period of extreme political and religious tension, associated with the expansion of

Sharia by the governments of different northern states within the Federal Republic of Nigeria, from 1999 onward."[14] That time of tension was partly the product of the weakening of the federal system of government in Nigeria, which ceded more power to individual states—states that were happy to intermingle religious authority with government. Many of these states had also been the focus of increased missionary activity by Wahhabist Muslims from the Gulf.

As a result, governors in these majority Muslim states also found (and still find) political support in accommodating increasingly conservative Nigerian Muslims.[15] Twelve of Nigeria's northern states are now governed by Sharia law.[16] While the 1999 revision of the Federal Republic of Nigeria's constitution didn't expand Sharia law per se, it further enshrined Islam within Nigeria's government so that the entire country feels as if it is effectually an Islamic state, even though only half of the nation is Muslim.

As one retired military officer first told us in secret during a visit, "The Constitution mentions Islam in some form many dozens of times, but despite this country being half Christian—and a kind of democracy—there isn't a single reference, or inference, related to Christianity."

Moreover, during the regime of current president Muhammadu Buhari's administration, the National Security Council and virtually all security agencies are led almost exclusively by northern Muslims.

This aggressive Islamization of the Nigerian state apparatus and key institutions also fuels conspiracy theories throughout the country, especially among Christians that "depict Boko

Haram as a front for other actors." In actuality, Boko Haram's leaders have "repeatedly rejected central symbols of Nigerian national identity [like] the constitution, the pledge of allegiance, the national anthem,"[17] and in February 2020, they threatened President Buhari when he visited Maiduguri days after the terrorists had murdered those thirty innocent civilians in Auno.[18]

It is troubling but true that on repeated occasions the Nigerian government attempted to negotiate with Boko Haram,[19] causing many inside and outside Nigeria to question why the government didn't simply crush the violent insurgent movement. Moreover, a West Point publication in 2012 struggled to explain why the Nigerian government wasn't doing more to deal with this radical insurgency, concluding that

> the Nigerian government seems incapable of responding to Boko Haram, and through a series of mistakes has revealed what outside observers have long suspected: certain elements of the security forces and political leaders of Muslim-majority northern Nigeria are either complicit with Boko Haram's operations, or they are taking a rather complacent view of its success.[20]

Complicit or not, one thing is clear: the Nigerian government will never be sufficiently "Islamic" to satisfy Boko Haram unless it becomes an Islamic state. Such a development could spawn horrors worse than what the world witnessed in Iraq and in Syria in 2014.

In fact, Boko Haram's leader, Abubakar Shekau, said as much even prior to the rise of ISIS in the Middle East. The occasion was a video message to Nigeria's former president Goodluck Jonathan (a Christian), who had called them a "cancer" after they bombed a church.

Shekau replied, "We are not a cancer. . . . The disease is unbelief. . . . [E]veryone knows democracy is unbelief, and everyone knows the constitution is unbelief, and everyone knows that there are things Allah has forbidden in the Qur'an . . . [things] that are going on in western schools."[21]

Along with the mounting Islamization of Nigeria, Boko Haram continues to wage an unrelenting war throughout the northeast of the country, razing villages, beheading "infidels," kidnapping young girls, and bringing every type of hell imaginable on earth. As we will soon see, these tactics particularly target Nigeria's vulnerable Christians. As Shekau brazenly declared in 2010, "We are declaring a holy war! We will fight the Christians, because everyone knows what they have done to the Muslims!"[22]

Boko Haram's brutality is increasingly outpaced by Fulani Muslim militants in other parts of Nigeria with a scorched earth methodology, even if the Fulanis do not fully share Boko Haram's theology or ideology.

They aren't alone either. Thousands of miles away, in East Africa, another group has similar sights set on Christians, moderate Muslims, and all Western influence.

YOU NEVER KNOW WHO IS AL-SHABAAB

In 2011, a Boko Haram suicide bomber launched a successful attack in the country's capital of Abuja. An attack on the capital of the country was enough to send shock waves throughout the rest of Nigeria. It also delivered a nasty surprise when the Nigerian intelligence services discovered that the "mastermind of the August 2011 suicide bombing . . . had received training in Somalia" from an al-Qaeda–affiliated group called al-Shabaab, after the Boko Haram leader had temporarily fled there from Nigeria in 2009.[23]

Like Boko Haram, Somalia's famous terrorists are multinational with a particular focus on Kenya, but they have struck as far away as Kampala in Uganda, where they killed seventy-four people in a single suicide attack in 2010.[24]

Al-Shabaab also enforces "a harsh interpretation of sharia, prohibiting various types of entertainment, such as movies and music; the sale of khat, a narcotic plant that is widely chewed in the region; smoking; and the shaving of beards. Stonings and amputations have been meted out to suspected adulterers and thieves."[25]

In a particularly profane demonstration of their inhumanity, "the group bans cooperation with humanitarian agencies, blocking aid deliveries as famine loomed in 2017. This forced some eight hundred thousand to flee their homes, according to the United Nations."[26]

This massively effective and destabilizing insurgency in Somalia began after the group's "first leader, Aden Hashi Ayro, received training in Afghanistan."[27] Here you see the global synergies among terrorists in obscure parts of the world. A jihadist in Afghanistan trained a Somali, who then trained a Nigerian. In each case there emerged ever-enlarging networks, eventually spreading murder, mayhem, and suffering to millions.

The roots of al-Shabaab go back to efforts by Osama bin Laden himself to train and fund extremists in Mogadishu. The terrorist group became a breakaway faction of a group originally funded and inspired by bin Laden. Al-Shabaab eventually emerged as the last such group standing in the aftermath of a war between the majority-Christian Ethiopia and Somalia. One counterterrorism expert observed at the Council on Foreign Relations that the Ethiopian conflict "transformed" al-Shabaab "from a small, relatively unimportant part of a more moderate Islamic movement into the most powerful and armed faction in the country."[28] The group continued to grow until "at its height, from around 2009 to 2010, Al Shabaab held [direct] sway over between 3 and 5 million people," observed BBC Africa editor Mary Harper.[29]

The fact that a single al-Shabaab truck bomb in Mogadishu killed 82 people in 2019 might sound shocking until you learn that in 2017 a single truck bomb killed more than 500. They also famously attacked the most important hotel in the city, killing many important officials just two weeks afterward.[30]

Their most spectacular and best-known attacks were at the luxury Westgate shopping mall in Nairobi, Kenya (2013), which killed nearly 70 people, and at the Garissa University College Garissa, Kenya (2015), which killed nearly 150. One shudders to think what such dedicated and ruthless killers could do if they ever got hold of weapons of mass destruction! It is deeply distressing that the common denominator of both murderous attacks was the terrorists hunting down Christians and executing them.

The *Guardian* reported an eyewitness account of the Westgate attack by a mall employee named Joshua Hakim, who hid underneath a table as the attack raged around him. He said that as he prayed, he recited a Christian phrase again and again. There were shots everywhere. Then two of the gunmen arrived on his level, and they yelled in English, "Muslims, get out of here!"

The story goes on: "Hakim approached one of the men, who was wielding an assault rifle in each hand [and he] showed the man his voter card, holding a thumb over his Christian name [Joshua]." They let him go, thinking he was a Muslim. Hakim heard them approach an Indian man, "[and he was] asked to name the mother of the prophet. When he hesitated, he was shot." As Hakim was running away, he witnessed an amazing and courageous Muslim woman take off her head covering, rip it in half, and give half of it to another woman, who wasn't a Muslim, so that she could cover her head.[31]

In Garissa four gunmen targeted mainly Christian students. In fact, they began their attack by targeting the school's 5:00 a.m. prayer meeting. One survivor said that "the militants went from room to room, asking if people were Christian or Muslim. If you were a Christian you were shot on the spot."[32]

From the beginning, part of Kenya's allure to al-Shabaab has been the goal of ridding the vast country of its majority Christian communities. In fact, in the spring of 2020—just as coronavirus was distracting the world—the group issued an "order" for every Christian across three counties in North Eastern Kenya to leave so that local Muslims could have their jobs and their property.[33] One of those was the county of Garissa.

Al-Shabaab's spokesperson Sheikh Ali Dhere said in a video posted online, "Muslim teachers, doctors, engineers, and young graduates from the northeastern province are unemployed. Isn't it better to give them a chance? There is no need for the presence of disbelievers."[34]

While the country and the world might have been shocked by the audacity of these militants, the local Christian communities were not. Since the 2013 attack on the Garissa University, the situation had been steadily deteriorating, with the murders of Christians occurring regularly. A local pastor was reported in the *Christian Post* as saying in response to al-Shabaab's order, "This is not news at all because the conduct of the local people here has always suggested that they want us to leave. This region has been unstable for years due to war in Somalia and hatred against . . . mostly Christians."[35]

The fact that the pastor alluded to the role of certain local Muslims in facilitating the insecurity in North Eastern Kenya is eerily similar to what one al-Shabaab informant told author Mary Harper about al-Shabaab–affiliated militants in Somalia:

It makes me think of a phrase I hear so often from Somalis: "Al Shabaab is everywhere and you never know who is Al Shabaab." It reminds me of the young boy from the coastal town of Brava, controlled for several years by the Islamists, who said, "Al Shabaab do not fall from the sky. They know us and we know them. They are our cousins, brothers, aunts and uncles."[36]

This phenomenon is akin to what we have observed in our conversations with Christian and Yazidi communities exiled from Mosul and villages across the Nineveh Plain by ISIS in 2014. They told us that in many circumstances, their neighbors "sold them out" or were silent as the terrorists moved in and offered them three options: convert, pay a tax, or die.

Of course there are many valiant stories of courageous and peace-loving Muslims who stood up to the terrorists to protect their neighbors. We think of the Muslims in North Africa who surrounded Egypt's churches when Muslim Brotherhood rioters attempted to attack those churches after the fall of Mohamed Morsi. But trust is increasingly hard to come by for beleaguered minorities who watched in dismay when neighbors could have done something yet chose not to.

Al-Shabaab's long arm has even reached into the United States. In 2009, more than two dozen Somali-Americans vanished from their community in Minneapolis. The FBI later determined they had been recruited to travel to Somalia to fight with al-Shabaab.[37]

Two

THE STRATEGY

*Osama bin Laden sent an aide to Nigeria
with about £1.8m in local currency to dispense
among groups that shared al-Qa'ida's
mission to impose Islamic rule. One of the
"major beneficiaries," the International
Crisis Group said, was Boko Haram.*
—TERRENCE MCCOY[1]

Mohammed's parents sat on the mud floor of their ramshackle home in Maiduguri, the capital of Nigeria's Borno State, holding the only two items they had to remind them of their dead son. The first was a certificate noting his graduation from junior secondary school, and the second was a single photo.

The photo shows a sixteen-year-old boy with bright eyes and a perfect smile. He looks kind, like a good son with a future as hopeful as his dreams.

Mohammed's father sat with his back slumped next to his wife, whose recessed eyes seem to be lost in a permanent state of shock and despair. Then he said something you'd never expect from looking at Mohammed's idealistic photo.

Breaking the cloud of silence hovering over the meeting, Mohammed's father suddenly declared, "There is nothing poverty cannot cause."

"Poverty, not ideology," Mohammed's father continued, drove his son to blow himself up to kill the innocent in the name of Boko Haram.[2] Mohammed wasn't the only one. A press release issued by UNICEF on August 22, 2017, read,

> UNICEF is extremely concerned about an appalling increase in the cruel and calculated use of children, especially girls, as "human bombs" in northeast Nigeria. Children have been used repeatedly in this way over the last few years and so far, this year, the number of children used is already four times higher than it was for all of last year. Since January 1, 2017, 83 children have been used as "human bombs"; 55 were girls, most often under 15 years old; 27 were boys, and one was a baby strapped to a girl.[3]

In Nigeria, Boko Haram's obsession with destroying Western education and influence has inspired them to target countless schools. By 2017, the terrorist group's insurgency in Borno State alone had forced more than three million children out of school, causing the closure of nearly 60 percent of the schools in the state.[4] Beyond Borno, in 2017, "some 10.5 million children are out of school throughout Nigeria . . . nearly 2300 teachers have been killed in Nigeria's northeast since 2009 . . . nearly 1400 schools have been destroyed."[5]

The numbers are staggering. The generational impact on Africa's present stability and future hope is incalculable. In Somalia, the home of al-Shabaab, nearly 60 percent of children live under the poverty line.

When we visited Nigeria together, we were shocked to discover that as many as one million children roam the streets of northeast Nigeria alone as the by-product of the terrorists' insurgency. This is in addition to the thousands of children intentionally raised to beg on the streets, including the three hundred found by Nigerian authorities in 2019, who were chained and tortured inside an Islamic school.[6] If Nigeria is a ticking time bomb, this lost generation of children could provide the kindling and fuses for the terrorists' goals.

TERRORISTS EXPLOIT POVERTY WHILE ISLAMISTS CREATE DEPENDENCY

Neither South Africa nor Egypt is the country with Africa's largest economy. It's Nigeria,[7] which has the tenth-largest oil reserve in the world, just above the United States.[8] Nigeria is also Africa's most populated country, with just over two hundred million people.[9] Yet, according to the World Data Lab's Poverty Clock, approximately 50 percent of Nigeria's total population lives in extreme poverty.[10] In 2018, Nigeria had the unfortunate distinction of overtaking India as the country with the world's most extreme poverty, with six people falling into extreme poverty every single minute.[11]

And Nigeria isn't alone. The Brookings Institution has predicted that on its current trajectory, the African continent will be home to 90 percent of the world's poorest people by 2030.[12] The poverty rate in Somalia's heartland, much of which is controlled by al-Shabaab, is a staggering 81 percent.[13]

Much of the world has shrugged its shoulders, even over the enormity of human suffering that these statistics reflect. But James Wolfensohn, a former president of the World Bank, has cautioned that there is another dimension to this real-time disaster: "We won't win the war against terror without addressing the problem of poverty."[14]

In one study of 450 former terrorists, including those who had joined Boko Haram, "employment" was the third-most cited reason for joining a terrorist group. Having a paying job was just behind "religious ideas" and "being a part of something bigger."[15] The study also analyzed what frustrations led the would-be terrorists to their cause. "Economic conditions" ranked just below "dissatisfaction with the state." A whopping 42 percent of the terrorist respondents admitted that they were given salaries for joining an extremist group.[16]

For example, one Islamic teacher in Abuja is struggling to make ends meet and provide for his wife and four children. This religious teacher told a reporter at the *Guardian* that his monthly salary was fifty dollars, and "even though school is free, we still need to pay examination fees and other costs. I go to the market to buy food every day. It costs me about $1.30 to feed eight people every day because I have other relatives living with me. It is very tough but I try to feed my family twice a day."[17]

We aren't inferring that this poor imam is a terrorist; of course he isn't. There are millions of entirely peaceful Muslims, including in the town in which Boko Haram originated, where a group of imams have been holding sessions to "persuade young people to not join Boko Haram."[18] We were also moved to learn that groups of Muslim and Christian leaders recently came together, calling for national prayer and fasting to promote "peace and love between the Muslims and Christians of Nigeria."[19] Also, at the height of the COVID-19 crisis, the sultan of Sokoto and the Nigerian Interreligious Council brought together Muslims and Christians to pray for their country.

But living on the edge of abject poverty spawns a sense of desperation—desperation born of want, desperation born out of a desire to make a difference for something bigger than oneself—easy pickings for terrorist recruiters with the cash and the certitude of their theological zeal. Thus it is no surprise that a leader of the Federal Neuropsychiatric Hospital told Al Jazeera that in this cauldron of poverty there are even instances of parents selling their children to the terrorists' cause.[20]

Large portions of countries such as Nigeria are, in effect, failed states within a state, which the government doesn't have either the capacity or the will to address. One imam, who is conducting counterextremism efforts in his community in Maiduguri, was more than willing to blame the principally Islamic Buhari administration: "There's a lot of poverty here and this is because of how the country is governed, some people feel marginalized."[21]

Such chronic poverty also lays bare the failure of governments to address their most basic responsibilities, leaving a gaping vacuum yearning to be filled. In Africa, this has opened the way for the likes of Boko Haram, ready to exploit and recruiting to supercharge their terrorist goals.

Elsewhere in Africa, other Islamists feeding off endemic poverty and corruption have fostered distrust among religious communities by creating ideological dependency and political loyalty with the goal of removing and replacing the existing ruling elite.

For instance, in addition to building countless schools that helped Islamize Egypt, the Muslim Brotherhood in 1977 began to provide inexpensive medical treatment throughout the country[22] in an effort to build a "parallel Islamic welfare sector" that would "advance their own politico-religious agenda."[23] In turn, "their legitimacy would then derive from their ability to provide for a counter project to the state's failure in development terms, and from the mobilization of Islamic values against the [government]."[24] That strategy worked in the Arab world's largest nation, and the Muslim Brotherhood swept into power from 2011 to 2013.

Such a strategy alarms many southern Nigerian Christians. They see Islamization steadily unfolding across the landscape of the North. In its most extreme form, this political technique has been dubbed "welfare terrorism" by researchers. They point to examples such as the efforts made by Egypt's

Muslim Brotherhood, the Gaza-based Hamas, and the Iranian Mullahcracy's terrorist lackeys in Lebanese Hezbollah. These are prime examples of sophisticated and successful game plans to gain the trust and loyalty of society's poorest sectors and to buy political loyalties en route to controlling political power.

> In recent decades, manifestations of this "welfare terrorism" have been numerous, from Hezbollah establishing schools, medical facilities, and agricultural schemes, to Hamas investing in educational, health and sociocultural infrastructures. In Afghanistan and Pakistan, the Taliban and Al-Qaeda have also employed such tactics by financing *madrassas* and educating the impoverished youth. Clearly, these various forms of "Islamist social welfare" have played a central role in the "growth and enduring popularity" of terrorist organizations in poor countries across the globe.[25]

Boko Haram hasn't succeeded in establishing an Islamic state as ISIS temporarily did in Iraq and in Syria between 2014 and 2015. The ISIS takeover resulted in the total destruction or hijacking of the institutions of the state and unspeakable death, destruction, and humanitarian crises. Instead, Boko Haram has used poverty to subsidize their ideological ranks with poor people for hire.

Take no solace that Boko Haram isn't yet in power. The steady Islamization of the northern states, which weakens the federal government in Nigeria, could be indicative of even worse things to come.

TERRORISTS UNDERMINE THE GOVERNMENT

As discussed previously, the British decided that the best way to manage Nigeria was to create a certain equilibrium between Islamic rule in the North—moderated by colonial influence—while installing total control elsewhere, utilizing Christian influence.

Historic Islamic conquests in the region, coupled with decisions by the British, laid the groundwork for a modern Nigerian society where religion is hopelessly intermingled with politics. This despite the constant refrain one hears in some Nigerian and Western quarters about problems having nothing to do with religion.

As a result, the proverbial elephant in the room is hardly ever addressed. Calls for recasting the nation's constitution go unheeded and, as a result, the nation has no stability, no accountability, no justice, and no national effort to confront terrorism. Extremists have often been able to blend into the Islamic North unnoticed by the rest of the world until the next horrific chapter is written. Even more alarming, some commentators don't view the evolution of Boko Haram as the advance of a terrorist group. In a piece published at the Brookings Institution, author Jideofor Adibe draws the conclusion that before 2009, Boko Haram's operations were "more or less peaceful," but it was radicalized in 2009, after a confrontation with Nigerian security agencies.[26]

To understand the absurdity of such an assertion, just listen to the incendiary rhetoric of the founder of Boko Haram, Mohammed Yusuf. He embraced extreme interpretations of Islam from the beginning, spent considerable time in Saudi

Arabia, and named the mosque he founded in Maiduguri after a famous thirteenth-century Salafi leader.[27]

In one sermon delivered openly in Maiduguri in 2006, Yusuf said,

> Once [the infidels] have power, once they have control, they show no mercy, they show no forgiveness. In Onitsha, they killed everyone. . . . That's why we can't put down our arms. Allah said: "You should always carry your weapons with you." Hide them! Allah didn't tell you to leave your weapons behind. Because if they gain an advantage over you, they won't spare you. You can't love them, you can't show them love, but you can show resistance. . . . A high-ranking officer will tell you: "We want peace and tranquility so we're going to protect you. We are Christians. They brought us here to protect you." But that's not true! In fact, he came to kill us, to hurt us.[28]

Boko Haram extends its definition of *infidel* to any Muslim who disagrees with their interpretation of Islam, as Yusuf's successor, Abubakar Shekau, said in a 2011 video: "Any Muslim who does not convert an atheist to Islam . . . but approves their way of life betrays Islam and is automatically expelled from Islam."[29]

Tragically, from its inception Boko Haram has pushed a religiopolitical agenda, which has aimed to "develop feelings of injustice" and "the stoking of hatred" while "calling for violence" against the government.[30]

Rather than crushing these extremists as armed insurgents, Nigerian authorities (especially the Buhari-led government) too often defer dealing with their security challenges, sidelining the pursuit of justice and stability. Instead, they cater to Islamist sensitivities, frequently choosing to negotiate[31] or even pay exorbitant ransoms.[32]

The clear but unspoken policy is not to rock the boat with Muslim constituents—even those who clearly oppose Boko Haram or ISIS in West Africa but are committed to Sharia, not democratic, law.

Take, for instance, the Sultan of Sokoto, who is the spiritual leader of Nigeria's Muslims—the twentieth such sultan since the eighteenth century.

Despite earning a reputation as a moderate, only in 2011 did the Sultan of Sokoto first utter a word about Boko Haram, and he chose to condemn a government crackdown on the group, saying, "We cannot solve violence with violence."[33]

In February 2020, at a conference on Countering Violent Extremism for Peaceful Coexistence, the sultan declared that the solution to dealing with Boko Haram is for Nigerians to "stop committing sin and abide by G-d's words."[34]

The Boko Haram terrorists and Fulani militants who have raided hundreds of Christian villages in the middle of the country see the government's reticence to act as a license to exploit constantly.

With a government that, by its repeated attempts to pay terrorist ransoms, shows no backbone to defeat terrorism, Boko Haram, ISIS in West Africa, certain Fulani militants, and others leverage that weakness to strengthen their brutal insurgency. They inspire more and more religious, impoverished jihadists to believe that their way is the just way, and their murderous tactics are paying off.

This isn't a new phenomenon, and the US and other Western democracies have poured billions in aid and support for a democratic Nigeria. But on the ground things have been quite different.

Johannes Harnischfeger, writing in 2006 about Fulani attacks against Christians in central Nigeria, said that "in Northern Nigeria, where some state governments have introduced a strict form of Sharia law, it is obvious that citizens are exposed to undue religious pressure. Muslim politicians use the police and other state institutions to enforce religious conformity within their own community and to marginalize the minority of non-Muslims."[35] In a section titled "The End of the Secular State," Professor Harnischfeger wrote,

When Nigeria returned to democracy in 1999 after fifteen years of military rule, the parliaments of twelve northern states enacted new laws meant to Islamise state and society. People in Europe learnt about it when a 35-year-old Nigerian woman was sentenced to stoning for extramarital sex. . . . The most severe consequences of the Sharia campaign seems to be that it has led to a confrontation between religious communities. . . . When the new legislation was introduced, the president of the Christian Association of Nigeria expressed his shock about this "irresponsible madness," and Professor Wole Soyinka, the Nigerian Nobel Laureate, assumed that it would be a "prelude to civil war." . . . Under Sharia, state authorities subsidize the building of mosques and pay the salaries of imams, while the religious activities of "infidels" are restricted.[36]

It is true that Boko Haram has killed both Muslims and Christians, and Buhari himself claims that 90 percent of Boko's victims have been Muslims.[37] But these figures are difficult to quantify based on available statistics and even the statements of the terror groups themselves. Surely no such murderers can be in actual service to G-d; it is also irresponsible to deny the religious component in the ongoing conflict and avoid confronting the key role that religion plays.

Despite all this, there's one reality-be-damned absurdity that both Muhammadu Buhari and his Christian predecessor, Goodluck Jonathan, embrace: both have insisted that the political conflict in Nigeria has "nothing to do with religion."[38]

You cannot defeat cancer without acknowledging the nature of the threat.

CREATE LOCAL CHAOS AND BROADCAST IT

As we will see through the voices of survivors in later chapters, Boko Haram and certain Fulani militants in the center of the country create chaos by terrorizing individual communities.

They arrive in trucks, with flags flying and machine guns shooting wildly into the air. In a Christian community, they may demand that the residents convert; if it's a mixed community, they will often separate the Muslims from the Christians, letting

the Muslims live while they massacre their Christian neighbors. They often torch cars and homes. One confidential list we
reviewed cited more than eighty churches destroyed by Boko
Haram in one area alone, along with many thousands of homes.

One researcher chronicled the militants' tactics by listing
dozens of suicide bombings and raids on towns and villages,
which sometimes were "carried out by just two or three gunmen on a motorcycle, some by hundreds of fighters supported by
tanks and anti-aircraft weapons mounted on flat-bed trucks."[39]
The terrorists would sometimes begin by targeting small police
or military institutions, and once those were subdued they would
capture the weapons and use them to attack civilians. Other
terrorists would roam around towns feigning insanity before
suddenly attacking.

They kidnap for ransom—by the thousands—but as we have
heard repeatedly, they often choose to kidnap Christians, freeing
anyone who can recite an Islamic creed. Victims often told us
that a terrorist kidnapping would take place a mile or less from a
police checkpoint—suspiciously close to the authorities.

It was chilling to hear of these Nazi-like death selections of
young Christian men and women, but this tactic has become
a lucrative business for the terrorists. Between 2016 and 2017,
according to the *Wall Street Journal*, the Nigerian president
authorized more than 3 million pounds to pay for the release of
103 Chibok girls whom Boko Haram had held hostage.[40]

Paying ransoms on this scale makes many Nigerians wonder
if the government is indirectly fueling the atrocities, and every
atrocity strengthens conspiracy theories based on one question:

If the government has the power to destroy the terrorists, why do they instead reward them with ransoms?

Others wonder if there are officials who may be getting a portion of the ransoms. This is a country rife with corruption that—aside from eroding justice and democratic institutions—in 2017 alone led to more than eighty million bribes in Nigeria, totaling $4.6 billion in purchasing power parity.[41]

Alarmingly, we are now seeing scores of Fulani militants in the Middle Belt of Nigeria attacking Christian villages by utilizing the same tactics—and sometimes more—used by Boko Haram. Incredibly, this brazen criminal and terrorist activity has generated roaring inaction—the sound of crickets—even as many of these attacks have taken place not far from the nation's capital of Abuja.

FOMENT TERROR THROUGH THE MEDIA

In 2015, President Buhari declared that Boko Haram was "technically defeated."[42] The following year he commended troops for "crushing the remnants of the Boko Haram insurgents."[43] In a nationally televised address in 2017, he said, "We have since beaten Boko Haram."[44] In 2019, the Nigerian president told the armed forces, "Boko Haram terrorists have been substantially defeated and degraded to the extent that they are only daring soft targets."[45] In another statement later in 2019, he said that "the real Boko Haram we know is defeated."[46]

During our visit in 2020, Buhari had visited Maiduguri to

show solidarity with thirty Nigerians who had been killed in the attack near Auno a few days earlier.

Nigeria's terrorists would never miss such an opportunity to spread more crippling fear; while Boko Haram's Abubakar Shekau cannot post his videos on YouTube anymore, that doesn't stop Nigerians and the international press from posting them. So when Shekau produced one, we saw its contents splashed across the front page of every newspaper in the country the next day. He said, "Buhari came to Maiduguri presenting to be a good man, but he is not. He shouldn't try to return to Maiduguri again. Buhari, fear your creator."[47]

Defeated indeed.

Three

CRIMINAL BANDITS OR JIHADI TERRORISTS?

Several times I note the proximity of a military
base that might have been expected to protect
civilians. But the soldiers didn't come; or,
if they did, it was only after the battle.

—BERNARD-HENRI LÉVY

Michael Nnadi was the kind of Nigerian whose face projected a nearly supernatural joy. His pronounced features made him look both older and younger than his eighteen years. His skin was dark, aglow with a smooth radiance that reflected the sun. An ever-present smile consumed his entire face, easily lighting up a room.

Michael was one of 270 students studying at the Good Shepherd Seminary in Kaduna State on the main highway to

Abuja. On the evening of January 8, 2020, his world was upended when an armed gang, disguised in military fatigues, breached the gate of the school. They snagged four seminarians, including Michael, and made their escape.[1]

The straightforward words of the seminary's registrar, Rev. Joel Usman, belied his anguish. "After [taking] the headcount of the students with security agents, four Seminarians have been declared missing. Kindly say a prayer for their release," Reverend Usman pleaded.[2]

Local authorities attributed the kidnappings to criminal activity by bandits whose interest was in whatever they could extort from the Catholic Church or the relatives of the four seminarians.

By the end of the month, three of the four boys had been freed, but not Michael. A few days later he was found dead, his body dumped on the side of a road, massacred by his kidnappers.[3]

It fell again to the registrar of the seminary to announce the horrific murder. "This is to inform all our friends and well-wishers that the remaining abducted Seminarian has been found dead. Thank you very much for your prayerful support." Reverend Usman added this plea: "Let us keep praying for Nigeria in great distress. . . . May the soul of our Brother Nnadi Michael and the souls of all the faithful departed rest in peace with the Lord. Amen."[4]

At Michael's funeral esteemed bishop Matthew Hassan Kukah of Sokoto denounced the injustice of his murder, trying to use the power of his words to awaken the conscience of a nation: "This is for us the moment of decision. This is the moment that separates darkness from light, good from evil. Our nation is like a ship stranded on the high seas, rudderless and with broken navigational aids. . . . Nigeria is on the crossroads, and its future stands precariously in a balance."[5]

Michael's twin brother, Raphael, spoke to the Nigerian press the week he and his brother would have turned nineteen. He saluted the path of spirituality, faith, and service that his brother had selected. "Michael was so much committed and loved the things of G-d, that his choice to become a priest did not surprise many people who knew him. My consolation is that he did not die in vain, pursuing things of the world, but rather he died in the service to G-d, training for the priesthood."[6]

It remained a mystery to Raphael, his family, and the seminary as to why Michael had been killed while the others had been freed. The same negotiators had been working on behalf of all four abductees. Some Nigerians, as well as local and international authorities, thought that he may have been disposed of as a negotiating tool to increase the ransom for the others, but no one knew for sure—until April 30, 2020.

That's the day the murderer, Mustapha Mohammed, was interviewed in prison by Nigeria's *Daily Sun* newspaper. The jailed gang leader detailed to the reporter that his gang took five days to survey the property, which was already familiar to one gang member who lived nearby. Then they attacked.

Mohammed spoke openly about Michael's fate, saying, "He did not allow me any peace; he just kept preaching to me his gospel."[7]

So why did Mohammed kill Michael?

"I did not like the confidence he displayed [in his faith], and I decided to send him to an early grave," said Mohammed.[8] This terrorist murderer is twenty-six years old and not a member of Boko Haram or ISIS in West Africa. He is a local Fulani Muslim and one of the forty-five members of a gang that has been working this area for years, brazenly kidnapping, extorting, and murdering the innocent.

The ransom they received for the other three abductees totaled about $25,000.

THE FULANI PROBLEM

Officials' initial refusal to attribute the attack in Kaduna to Islamists—in any form—reflects a black hole of denial that is pronounced in Nigerian politics. This endemic self-censorship has been absorbed by many professionals in the foreign policy establishment who have been tracking and analyzing developments in Nigeria. There is a bias to avoid the religious components of these outrages at all costs to prevent being accused of politicizing religion. This denial serves as an accelerant of religion-fueled conflict—until the facts and blood on the ground can no longer be denied.

Accelerant is the word the United States ambassador to Nigeria, Mary Beth Leonard, used in our meeting in February 2020. We asked her about the religious aspects of the violence and conflict in the heart of the country. She denied it was at all about religion and described the conflict as "fundamentally a resource issue." Religion was, according to Ambassador Leonard, only relevant as it served as a potential *accelerant* to conflict. She left us with the impression that people like us, by speaking up for victims of religious persecution, were a part of the problem. We found this to be hugely alarming.

Later we looked at the embassy's public statements and social media accounts and discovered that they said almost nothing about the conflict, let alone any of its religious components. We found Ambassador Leonard's perspective particularly disheartening, given that she serves a secretary of state whose foreign policy has held little ambiguity as to the role of religion in the conflict and the essentialness of protecting religious freedom in Africa's largest country.

Of course, no one disagrees about the need to depoliticize religion in Nigeria. Even Aid to the Church in Need (ACN), an international Catholic aid organization, addressed whether the Kaduna attack was religiously motivated, using these carefully selected words: "According to ACN, there has been no indication of the abduction being religiously motivated *up to now*"[9] (emphasis ours). Yet in this same statement, five days following the attack, they rightly left open the door for subsequent information to come to light and further noted:

> What is [also] concerning is the security situation of the whole of Nigeria's so-called Middle Belt—which includes Kaduna. The situation is already extremely precarious owing to the numerous and repeated attacks on mainly Christian villages by members of the nomadic Fulani people. Thousands of people have lost all their properties and been left as refugees.

> At the same time, [the] Islamist Boko Haram terrorist group
> has continued to perpetrate its atrocities across the northeast
> of the country.[10]

They were right to leave this door for further information open because Michael was killed not for *money* but—in the precise words of his killer—solely because of his *faith*.

Should it surprise anyone that a young Fulani Muslim, who was also a thug, would become so incensed by the faith of his Christian neighbor? After all, many of the atrocities being committed in Nigeria today occur not only at the hands of Boko Haram terrorists in the Northeast but at the hands of Fulani militants in the heart of the country, not far from its capital. This Middle Belt is populated by both Christians and Muslims and serves as a de facto dividing line between the predominantly Islamic North and predominantly Christian South.

Those who survived one of the hundreds of surprise attacks on Christian communities here (including everyone we personally interviewed) recounted that the Fulani militants were yelling "Allahu Akbar" as they attacked—before they stole the land, cattle, and other resources.

These attacks are clearly enabled by a kind of Islamic supremacy, which makes the attackers feel entitled to Christian property, akin to what previous generations of Fulani Muslim raiders believed when initially establishing their foothold in Northern Nigeria two hundred years ago. In fact, the Sokoto Caliphate itself was established through an Islamic jihad in the early nineteenth century, and its leaders were "most, but not all . . . ethnic, Fulani."[11] Expansionist efforts by Fulani jihadists have continued for generations, and similar raids are being deployed today.[12]

While these Fulani attacks are distinct from Boko Haram, their tactics are eerily similar. Virtually every Christian, and many Muslims, concede that these Muslim militants—while having a long history of jihadism—have been emboldened by Boko Haram, even if they aren't aligned with the latter's political insurgency.

The French intellectual and human rights activist Bernard-Henri Lévy traveled throughout the Middle Belt in late 2019 to focus exclusively on the Fulani raids against Christian communities. In a *Wall Street Journal* essay reflecting on his visit, published days before Hanukkah and Christmas that year, Lévy wrote:

> A slow-motion war is under way in Africa's most populous country. It's a massacre of Christians, massive in scale and horrific in brutality. And the world has hardly noticed.
>
> A Nigerian Pentecostal Christian, director of a nongovernmental organization that works for mutual understanding between Nigeria's Christians and Muslims, alerted me to it. "Have you heard of the Fulani?" . . . The Fulani are an ethnic group, generally described as shepherds from mostly Muslim Northern Nigeria, forced by climate change to move with their herds toward the more temperate Christian South. They number 14 million to 15 million in a nation of 191 million.
>
> Among them is a violent element. "They are Islamic

extremists of a new stripe," the NGO director said, "more or less linked with Boko Haram."[13]

In the first three months of 2020, more than four hundred civilian Christians were killed in Fulani raids and hundreds of homes burned.[14] On our visit we were supposed to meet with a representative from one of these villages. Instead, the leaders of the entire village came, filling up our hotel room, with the adult men still bearing a look of total shock on their faces even though the attack had occurred many weeks before.

They described the Fulani raiders arriving under the cover of darkness with their jihadist chants and their AK-47s. The marauders swiftly maimed and murdered Christians while burning down every structure and pillaging what remained.

Hundreds of similar incidents have occurred. We reviewed one confidential list that precisely documents attacks by Fulani militants on seventy-nine Christian villages over the last five years *in one state alone.* Yet we haven't identified a single case where the perpetrators were brought to justice or where security forces prevented an attack.

Survivors recount that all these attacks were punctuated by jihadi calls. Nevertheless, countless policy makers, scholars, and diplomats refuse to acknowledge that the Fulani attackers are at least partially inspired by Islamic extremism. In fact, in 2018, when Fulani raiders massacred eighty-six Christians and burned fifty homes around Jos, the Associated Press headline read, "86 Killed in Nigeria as Farmers, Herders Clash."[15] A similar report in *Time* magazine included a photo of a large Christian funeral but didn't mention the words *Christian* or *Muslim* and, instead, simply described the conflict this way: "Bloody clashes between farmers and nomadic herders in Nigeria's central Plateau State in late June claimed at least 86 lives, as each group vied for the region's increasingly scarce farmland."[16] The reporter attributed the cause of the attacks to "climate change." CNN reported that the incident had the "potential to exacerbate ethnic tensions in an increasingly volatile region."[17]

Denying the religious element in Nigeria's conflict defies credulity. We are writing to nullify this immoral status quo; the time has come to demand that those who promote this accepted narrative prove that religion plays no role in the ongoing slaughter.

Even efforts to acknowledge the complexity and nuance of the conflict won't do. Take what John Campbell, a senior fellow at the Council on Foreign Relations, wrote in 2019:

> When Christians or Muslims are killed in the Middle Belt, it is not clear exactly why. Is it because they are a farmer or a herder? Or because they are ethnically Fulani, many of whom are herders, or of a small ethnic group, who are often farmers? Or is it because they are Muslims, which most Fulani are, or Christian, which those of many small ethnic groups are? These questions are not easily answered.[18]

Perspectives such as Dr. Campbell's unintentionally befog the facts on the ground and allow the world to avert its eyes from the perpetrators of ethnic cleansing. After all, there are virtually no Christian raids on Fulani to report. We were able to identify only one incident when the Christians under attack were even able to defend themselves. This is a one-sided, violent campaign, with the Fulani attacking the innocent in the dead of night.

The rare incidents of Christians attacking Fulani herders happened in retaliation to an initial attack by Fulanis, and there are almost no incidents of Fulani herders attacking Christian farmers without the accompanying jihadist cry of "Allahu Akbar!" More often than not, the Christians are taken as lambs to a slaughter.

In an attempt to avoid blame for striking the kindling of a holy war, too many so-called experts would rather twist their analyses into verbal pretzels than acknowledge that this is a deadly religious persecution that demands the world's attention and action. Nigeria has a religious freedom problem and a human rights problem, not just a problem of natural resources and poverty.

The truth is that the conflict is increasingly a religious conflict with the other elements actually serving as the "accelerants" (read: "excuses and justifications"). It has all worsened by the government failing again and again at its core responsibility, the responsibility of any government: to first and foremost protect its citizens.

We only wish that academic residents safely ensconced in their ivory towers would take the time to come face-to-face with the victims. Let those scholars then debate what those armed militants were thinking before they barged into another Christian town yelling, "Allahu Akbar!" with their AK-47s firing.

Could those thugs really be thinking, *I want their land because climate change has taken mine*? Or just maybe they are thinking, *G-d is fine with my attacking these people because, as I have been taught, G-d entitles me to the property of these infidels, including their beautiful girls.*

Whatever the cause—whether the Fulani are violent criminals or jihadi terrorists—there is one indisputable fact: the Nigerian government is failing to stop the bloodshed, and the apathy of the international community is aiding and abetting their indifference.

DEADLY DÉJÀ VU? THE SAME "EXPERTS" DIDN'T DESIGNATE BOKO HARAM

The present debate over the motivation for the Fulani raids also brings a sense of foreboding to observers who believe that earlier direct action by the United States against Boko Haram could have curtailed the catastrophic results of the conflict while saving many lives. But in 2013, the Department of State relentlessly and absurdly resisted designating Boko Haram as a foreign terrorist organization—despite intense pressure from the FBI, Department of Justice, and Department of Homeland Security.[19]

During a congressional hearing in 2012, Representative Bob Turner described why he thought the Department of State's resistance was absurd: "There is a bill in the Senate [to do so]. There is a bill in the House. This group has attacked the U.N.

There have been over 1,000 deaths attributed to it. Their attacks have been very pointed on religious grounds, on Christmas, on Easter, attacking Christian churches . . . [yet] it has been blocked by the State Department."[20]

Johnnie Carson, assistant secretary of state for African affairs from 2009 to 2013, responded at the hearing that he wasn't an expert on the issue, and he would have to get back to the committee.

Assistant Secretary Carson actually *did* have opinions on the issue. On "the day after [an Easter Sunday] Nigeria church bombing" in 2012, Carson told a forum at the Center for Strategic and International Studies in Washington, DC, that "religion is not driving extremist violence in . . . northern Nigeria."[21] He went on to describe what the United States was doing to combat the escalating violence in the country:

> We have provided technical assistance to support reform in the power sector. We have taken a large energy trade mission to the country, and encouraged the swift passage of a strong petroleum industry bill that brings more transparency to the sector. We have recognized the importance of Nigeria's agriculture sector and supported Nigeria's comprehensive agriculture development plans. And in the health sector, we have committed over $500 million a year to the President's Emergency Plan for AIDS Relief, demonstrating how critical we consider Nigeria in the worldwide fight against HIV and AIDS.[22]

All of those are important initiatives and laudable efforts by the United States, but what of the security situation?

Reflecting on Carson's remarks, Hudson Institute's Nina Shea noted that he "made a point of stating that U.S. policy was to press Nigeria to 'de-emphasize the role of the military.'"[23] The bottom line, according to the State Department's number one official for Africa, was that the United States wasn't interested in the Nigerian military taking out the terrorists.

Several years later Carson doubled down in an interview with the *New York Times*, stating that the Department of State had "opposed making the designation 'for six or seven different reasons.'"[24] What were those reasons?

The article recounted some of them. "Carson said he was concerned that the move would generate publicity for the group and help it attract support from other extremists. He said he was also worried that the designation might legitimize a heavy-handed crackdown by Nigeria's security forces at a time when American officials were urging them to avoid human rights abuses."[25]

So the official policy of the United States government was to "disincentivize" Nigeria's security services from taking out Boko Haram. The message was to essentially ignore them and to work on addressing poverty, climate change, and other inequalities in the region rather than to directly confront, degrade, and destroy the terrorist insurgency incubating in Africa's largest and wealthiest country.

Eventually, and only after both US Secretary of State Hillary Clinton and her assistant secretary Johnnie Carson had departed, did the State Department designate Boko Haram a "foreign terrorist organization."[26]

NOT EVERY FULANI IS A JIHADIST

Understanding that the Fulani represent "the largest semi-nomadic group in the world and are found across West and Central Africa—from Senegal to the Central African Republic"[27]—is fundamental. In Nigeria alone there are nearly seventeen million Fulani.[28]

While the perpetrators of violence in the Middle Belt are almost exclusively Fulani, the vast majority of Fulani are not perpetrators. Indeed, many Fulani Muslims have spoken out against them. And other Fulani have also been killed by Islamist terrorists throughout the country, including during a terrible attack on a mosque in the Northeast in 2018,[29] and another brazen attack that targeted three emirs from the Northeast, killing one in 2014.[30]

Therefore, observers and activists must be cautious about automatically drawing an ideological line between the number of Fulanis in Buhari's administration, including Buhari himself, and the government's inaction against the perpetrators of mayhem and violence. Minus explicit evidence, other Nigerians simply cannot draw such conclusions without fanning the flames of xenophobia.

Nevertheless, the Nigerian government has serious challenges it can no longer ignore. What is their response to the charges laid by a former defense minister in a 2018 lecture?

"The armed forces are not neutral. They collude with the armed bandits to kill people, kill Nigerians." He added that they "facilitate" their movement; they cover them. "If you wait for the armed force to stop the killing, you all die one by one. The ethnic cleansing must stop . . . otherwise, Somalia will be a child's place."[31]

His condemnation would never have been uttered if Fulani leaders themselves—including Nigeria's president—more clearly, more frequently, and more loudly condemned these attacks and pledged to protect their Christian neighbors by deploying the personnel and resources to defend the Christian communities from these violent marauders. At this advanced stage, however, words alone will be rendered meaningless without action to stop the evil and save the innocent.

What kind of action could stem the tide? Look no further than one imam. When Fulani attackers "launched coordinated attacks on Christian farmers in 10 villages" in central Nigeria's Plateau State in June 2018, eighty-three-year-old cleric and imam Abubakar Abdullahi hid Christians.[32] In fact, he did more than just hide them:

> As Imam Abdullahi was finishing midday prayers, he and his congregation heard gunshots and went outside to see members of the town's Christian community fleeing. Instinctively, the Imam ushered 262 Christians into the mosque and his home next to the mosque. The Imam then went outside to confront the gunmen and he refused to allow them to enter, pleading with them to spare the Christians inside, even offering to sacrifice his life for theirs.[33]

That mosque, which he had served in for sixty years, was built on land originally gifted by the Christian community to their Muslim neighbors.[34] The imam survived, as did all 262 Christians.

THE GOVERNMENT MUST DECIDE

When the news of Michael Nnadi's martyrdom emerged, the archbishop of Lagos, Most Rev. Alfred Adewale Martins, was enraged. "This is just one of several cases of innocent Nigerians being killed daily by kidnappers while our security services and their chiefs watch as if they were helpless." He continued:

> Recently we recorded the case of [a Christian beheaded] in Adamawa State . . . and before that the murder of eleven innocent people. . . . Also, the situations of suicide bombers going into mosques to murder people who had gone to worship. . . . This appalling situation must come to an end.
>
> Nigerians cannot just fold our arms and allow these monstrous activities to continue to thrive. The Buhari-led Government must act now before things get out of hand.
>
> . . . The utilization of [kid gloves] approach by the security agencies in addressing insecurity in the land is not producing the desired result.[35]

Bernard-Henri Lévy felt similarly after traveling through

the parts of Nigeria where Fulani militants raided Christian communities:

> Several times I note the proximity of a military base that might have been expected to protect civilians. But the soldiers didn't come; or, if they did, it was only after the battle; or they claimed not to have received the texted SOS calls in time, or not to have had orders to respond, or to have been delayed on an impassable road.
>
> "What do you expect?" our driver asks as we take off in a convoy for his burned-down church. "The army is in league with the Fulani. They go hand in hand."[36]

One victim told Lévy that "[after one attack] we even found a dog tag and a uniform."[37]

Four

AN IMPROBABLE JOURNEY
TO FAITH AND FREEDOM

> *Having heard all of this you may choose*
> *to look the other way but you can*
> *never again say you did not know.*
> —William Wilberforce,
> House of Commons, 1791

In the early nineteenth century, Fulani and Yoruba Muslim raiders kidnapped Ajayi from his hometown in western Nigeria, in the modern state of Oyo. He was only thirteen years old, and the raiders likely swept up the entire village that disastrous day. Ajayi's fate wasn't uncommon for young people unfortunate enough to be born in this terrible time in history: "From the last third of the 16th century to the early 19th centur[y], Portuguese, then Dutch, then French and English merchants greedily expanded the African slave trade internationally. . . . Over this period of trade, more than 3.5 million slaves were shipped from Nigeria to North and South America and the Caribbean colonies."[1]

The slave trade was enormously profitable for the traders, "mostly [for] Europeans, but a small number of Africans also benefited economically, mostly along the southwestern coast of Nigeria."[2] Who was included in that "small number of Africans" who benefited? Slave traders within the Fulani and Yoruba Muslim tribes.

Like most slaves, Ajayi was sold several times until he eventually ended up in the possession of Portuguese slave traders who loaded him onto a ship to cross the Atlantic.[3]

This is when fate suddenly took a positive turn. While they hadn't outright banned the practice of slavery yet, the British had banned the slave trade in 1807. The ban was partly attributed to the "growth of evangelical Protestantism in the late 1700s [which] lent a critical voice to discussions of slavery."[4] This movement that helped lead to the total abolition of slavery in the British Empire was most famously encapsulated in the work of the great abolitionist William Wilberforce. Saving slaves became Wilberforce's lifework, and his most stirring words on the evils of slavery and the imperative to abolish the institution were delivered on the floor of the House of Commons in 1791, where he declared, "Having heard all of this you may choose to look the other way but you can never again say you did not know."[5]

It took another sixteen years before slave trade was banned in the British Empire and forty-two years before slavery was finally abolished—the same year the crusading Wilberforce died.

Ajayi might have ended up a slave in America, but the Portuguese ship he was on ran into a vessel from the British Royal Navy, which by this time had begun "policing the coast, intercepting slave ships and releasing their prisoners."[6] The British took over the slave ship and its human cargo. Ajayi and the other captives were taken to Freetown, Sierra Leone, where he was granted his freedom.[7]

There Ajayi eventually became Christian. He changed his name to Samuel Ajayi Crowther after joining the church that had taken him in when he arrived in that strange new country with nothing to his name except his newfound freedom. The church had fed and clothed him, taught him English, and educated him more broadly.

Eventually Crowther became a bishop of the Anglican Church and was stationed in England before the former slave returned to his native Nigeria as the first African Anglican bishop.[8]

Preceding Crowther in returning to Nigeria were hundreds of other freed slaves led by twenty-three who had chosen to leave Sierra Leone for Nigeria instead of England "to proclaim, in a center of the slave trade over 1000 miles off" a Christianity that "they trusted would sweep away the odious [slave trade]."[9] Petitioning the British government to allow them to go, they wrote:

> Your humble petitioners are Liberated Africans, and we feel . . . thankful to Almighty G-d and the Queen of England, who had rescued us from being in a state of slavery . . . so we take upon ourselves to direct this our humble petition to your

Excellency. That the Queen will graciously sympathize with her humble petitioners to establish a colony to Badagri that the same may be under the Queen's Jurisdiction, and beg of her Royal Majesty to send missionar[ies] with us and by so doing the slave trade can be abolished . . . so that the gospel . . . can be preached throughout our land.[10]

Their request was granted. As early as the fifteenth century, foreign Catholic missionaries had attempted and failed to Christianize Nigeria, but the power of these native-born messengers, who had been forcibly exiled to suffer the indignity and inhumanity of slavery, started a spiritual movement that would eventually make Nigeria the country with the largest Christian population in the whole of Africa.

Chief among them was Samuel Ajayi Crowther. He eventually was asked to come lead the growing Christian enterprise founded by his freed compatriots. Upon returning to Nigeria, Crowther also miraculously found his mother after having been separated for twenty-five years. That day he penned these words in his diary:

[The Bible says] "thou art the helper of the fatherless." I have never felt the force of this text more than I did this day. . . . [W]hen [my mother] saw me she trembled. She could not believe her eyes. We grasped one another, looking at one another in silence and great astonishment, while the big tears rolled down her emancipated cheeks. She trembled as she held me by the hand and called me the familiar names, which I well remember I used to be called by my grandmother, who had since died in slavery. We could not say much but sat still, casting many an affectionate look toward each other. . . . I cannot describe my feelings. I had given up all hope and now after a separation of twenty-five years, without any plan or device of mine, we were brought together again.[11]

Crowther and his followers soon met vicious persecution in Nigeria, though. At first it came from a controversy surrounding Christian burial practices that were impacting revenues of the local religious communities that handled traditional burial rites. The businessmen provoked a riot, leading to Christians being nearly beaten to death before being "abandoned in the open, where for five days, they were scorched by the sun and beaten by the rain."[12]

The worst of the persecution came from the profiteering and "slave-trading king, Kosoko," who was in Lagos. King Kosoko was not a Muslim, but he considered the new Christian activity in the region to be "the greatest threat to the slave trade," and he thought it "could succeed."[13] Kosoko was correct. These Christian activists would become his worst nightmare.

It took Crowther visiting England, where he traveled throughout the country speaking against the vices of Kosoko, to awaken the conscience of Britain sufficiently to provoke British intervention in Lagos.

[After] two days of fighting, Kosoko's forces were subdued . . . [and] on January 1, 1852, Akintoye, the new king, signed a treaty with the British government "for the abolition of the traffic in slaves, the encouragement of legitimate trade, and the protection of missionaries." . . . [T]he section of the treaty which concerned Christian(s) [said], "they shall not be hindered . . . in their endeavors . . . or troubled in any manner whatsoever."[14]

Thus was the beginning of the Christian presence in Nigeria. Eventually it would attract every Christian denomination and countless adherents of every type. In the last half century evangelical and pentecostal Christianity burst onto the scene, leading to the establishment of some of the largest churches in the world. And "apart from . . . souls, one of the first major fruits of missionary labour in Nigeria was Western education."[15]

To be clear, while Christianity's arrival and spread throughout Nigeria might have been linked to colonial powers, the spiritual flag of Christianity in Nigeria was planted by local former slaves for whom freedom and Christian faith were deeply intertwined.

Today a different type of slavery still vexes Nigeria.

BRING BACK OUR GIRLS

In April 2014, Boko Haram targeted the primarily Christian town of Chibok in Borno State. By the time the terrorist siege was over, 276 girls were kidnapped from a government secondary boarding school, sparking global outrage punctuated by a viral social media campaign marked by the hashtag #BringBackOurGirls.[16]

Helon Habila, noted Nigerian writer and George Mason University professor, traveled to Chibok to interview eyewitnesses of that terrible night for his book *The Chibok Girls*. Among those eyewitnesses was Rev. Philip Madu, whose reflection stemmed from the simple prompt, "Tell me about the night of the kidnapping":

Around 5:30 p.m. to 6:00 p.m. that day, I had a call saying there were rumors that they [Boko Haram] were coming to attack Chibok. . . . That day my wife wasn't around, just the children and me. Well, around 10:00 p.m. or quarter to 11:00 p.m., I heard pa-pa-pa-pa, gunshots. I woke up the kids. We were sleeping out here in the yard. It was April and very hot.

We heard the gunshots, going on and on. We ran out of town and hid. . . . [The attack] went on for hours. They started around 11:00 p.m.; they didn't finish until around 2:00 a.m.

Well, in the morning . . . when we went to the school we saw the girls' clothes and uniforms scattered all over the place. Parents started crying, but there was nothing they could do. There was no word from the government or any person in authority. The next day the parents said they just couldn't sit still and do nothing while their girls were being taken away. They said they'd rather die pursuing them.

The men formed a group and went after them. They entered the bush and got to a village in Damboa that local government called Njaba, when the villagers saw them. They asked them if they were the parents of those girls, and they said yes. They said, "These men are not too far ahead of you, but our advice is we don't think you will come back alive if you keep following them. What is the point in losing your life as well as that of your daughters? Better go back."

They took two of my brother's daughters. . . . Up to now we haven't received any news of them.[17]

A Nigerian mother of one of the Chibok girls also recounted her memory of that terrible night:

It was an awful night, April 14, 2014. We had no information, no idea, no news, nothing. We just heard gunshots coming from the direction of her boarding school.

Lord, my daughter! All my knowledge, my brain, my head, my strength, my energy went out to that school. We had heard they planned to attack schools and kidnap kids. I called my sister. She didn't know anything.

She said, "Just give up for the night." But I said, "I [am] going to the school for my baby!" My husband stopped me. He said, "There is security in the school."

But I could hear the gunshots, so I planned to go fight. I grabbed some rocks because we have rocks everywhere.

There were normally fourteen or fifteen security soldiers. But they could not win. We don't know what happened.

The girls were gone. We saw their uniforms, their dresses, everything scattered everywhere. We thought the girls had tried to escape or the security had rescued them or something of that nature. But the whole school was burned. They destroyed the roof. They burned out everything.

We met one girl, and I asked her, "Where are the girls?" She said, "I don't know."

I kept crying, "Where is my baby?" I called her name.

After an hour or two, some girls came walking toward the school. We rushed to them and said, "What's happened?" They said, "Boko Haram has kidnapped and packed up all of them."

"How did they pack them up?" I asked. . . .

The escaped girls said they packed them in trucks and cars and carted them away. It was a government-run "comprehensive boarding school," so the boys went in the morning for the lectures. In the evening, after closing hours, the boys would go home.

But the girls stayed in the dormitory. So the boys were secured because they were home with their parents. But the girls . . . the girls . . . that happened to them! I talked to many girls. Many girls. I tried to sort out where my baby was. I have a cousin who was with her, who escaped. She said my daughter was in the truck close to the driver. She couldn't escape.

My baby was not yet sixteen, but now she is eighteen. She was writing her final paper. I don't know where she might be. I am hoping that one day we will see them. Prayer is the only key to success. With G-d, it is possible. He is a great G-d. My baby . . . [18]

Reverend Madu recounted what he had learned from the few girls who had escaped. Boko Haram militants had arrived at the boarding school dressed in military uniforms. In a cruel and insidious tactic reminiscent of how Nazis often deceived Jews before deporting them to ghettos or death camps, these terrorists dressed as soldiers convinced the girls to quietly go with them to get them out of harm's way from approaching Boko Haram.

As a result, they succeeded in getting 276 young girls to gather quietly in a single place before loading them calmly onto a large truck that drove away to "protect them."[19]

Those Chibok girls became slaves of different sorts to their terrorist masters, especially through forced marriages to Boko Haram militants. One escapee explained that when several of the girls refused to be married, "they came back to us with four men, they slit their throats in front of us. They then said that this will happen to any girl that refuses to get married."[20] The same woman also told the BBC that she was then repeatedly raped, and "there was so much pain . . . I was only there in body . . . I couldn't do anything about it."[21] And if this wasn't bad enough, the terrorists forced some of the other girls to slit the throats of captive "Christian men. They forced the Christians to lie down. Then, the girls cut their throats."[22]

The girls who initially escaped from Boko Haram survived only because of the kindness of Fulani tribesmen who sheltered them and provided for them until they could find their way home, proving—yet again—a warning that one cannot fall prey to demonizing an entire group because of the evil committed by some. The majority of the Fulani in Nigeria who are not militant are a peace-loving people. There are those who are Muslims and those who are not, and they are also targets of those radicals who have embarked upon a vicious mission to ethnically cleanse Nigeria of Christian communities.

You might think that such a brazen attack with all the global interest and notoriety it spawned would have made the government provide effective security for this part of Borno State. But you would be mistaken. Just seven months after those girls were abducted, Boko Haram returned again to Chibok. Reverend Madu describes that day as well:

> I remember, we were in church that day, me and my wife and my three small children. Around 3:45 p.m., we were having our Bible study. . . . We heard the gunshots, pa-pa-pa-pa-pa. . . . The church members stood up to leave, but I told them, "No, let's pray first and ask for G-d's guidance." After prayer, before I could lock the church doors, bullets had started flying everywhere. We took the [motorcycle] and started for the bush. . . . [We] returned to Chibok on Tuesday, but the children couldn't sleep at night.[23]

In this incident Boko Haram didn't destroy the community's church, but for some reason they chose to destroy something inside of it—a picture of Jerusalem that Reverend Madu had brought with him back to Chibok after a once-in-a-lifetime pilgrimage in 2007.[24]

THEN THERE WAS LEAH

At the time of this writing, more than one hundred of the Chibok girls are still missing. Others escaped or were freed after the federal government paid ransom money and agreed to exchange Boko Haram prisoners for Chibok girls. Yet the sense of crisis and quiet rage persists six years later.

What has been missed in much of the coverage is that the Chibok girls were mainly Christians, and those Christian girls also faced the prospect of forced conversion.[25] This was the case with one of the 110 young girls who were similarly kidnapped in February 2018 from the Government Girls' Science and Technical College in the town of Dapchi, in Yobe State.[26]

Yes, it happened again.

Reuters reported, "Some of the attackers were camouflaged, with witnesses stating that a number of students thought they were soldiers."[27] Despite Boko Haram having threatened this part of Nigeria for so many years, the press reported nonchalantly that, in the aftermath of this attack, "police and security officials had been deployed to schools in the state."[28]

The Nigerian government clearly knew something of the whereabouts of the terrorists, because just one month later all but six of the girls were released when the government paid millions of dollars to ransom them.[29] Five of those who didn't return to their parents died, reportedly by accident, in transit when they were being abducted. The sole living schoolgirl who didn't return was Leah Sharibu. Today she has emerged as one of the most famous victims in the entire world. Leah was the only Christian among the 110 girls who had been kidnapped in Dapchi.[30]

The day the other girls were released, Leah's parents weren't told by the government that she wasn't among them. The

Guardian reported, "Rebecca Sharibu, the mother of Leah, 15, heard girls' voices and the sound of vehicles driving past her house. She was told to stay inside, but when she heard the cars coming back after dropping the girls off, she ran out. All around her were joyful parents and their returned daughters. But, she could not find Leah anywhere."[31]

Mrs. Sharibu only found out the fate of her daughter when she asked two of Leah's friends, "Where is Leah, I can't find my Leah, why did you leave her there?"[32]

Leah's friends replied, "Boko Haram told Leah to accept Islam and she refused. So they said she would not come with us. . . . [W]e begged her to just recite the Islamic declaration and put the hijab on and get into the vehicle, but she said it was not her faith, so why should she say it was? If they want to kill her, they can go ahead, but she won't say she is a Muslim."[33]

A FRIENDSHIP WORTH HAVING

We visited Nigeria two years to the day after Leah's kidnapping. On the morning of the day we were scheduled to meet with the Nigerian government at the presidential enclave, President Buhari issued the following statement:

Two years ago, 110 innocent children from the town of Dapchi were taken, against their will, by the terrorists of Boko Haram. . . . Today all but one—Leah Sharibu—are returned to their families. Now aged 16, Leah remains in the hands of the terrorists—they say because she refuses to renounce her Christian faith. We say, as the government for and of all Nigerians, that no person has the right to force another to change their faith against their will and that all life is sacred. This government continues and seeks to secure the release of all children and captives of terrorists—and we do so regardless of their creed or the name of their creator. As we redouble our efforts for Leah's return, we can never allow the terrorists to divide us—Christian against Muslim, Muslim against Christian. We are all Sons of Abraham. And all Nigerians have the same worth and rights before the law, and before G-d.[34]

Powerful and appropriate words from the nation's leader. Tragically, they have yet to lead to action that would free Leah from slavery and reunite her with her family.

All of the 104 remaining Muslim girls abducted in Dapchi were recovered within one month, but the 112 Christian girls from Chibok have not been released. These are reasons why some Christians view with suspicion President Buhari's ruling coalition of Fulani Muslims with Yoruba Muslims. Add to this a common sentiment that Nigeria's nationwide syndicate of abductions is Fulani-run, and it all undermines any sense of trust in religious freedom or equal rights.

On April 14, 2020, six years to the day after the Chibok girls were kidnapped in Borno State, the *Wall Street Journal* reminded the world of their terrible fate, especially those among the 112 who are still missing.

The article included a subtitle underscoring the insecurity

in Nigeria. It alluded to the possibility of future danger for the Chibok girls who had been fortunate enough to be freed, because "a rise of attacks in Nigeria . . . [raises] a grim prospect: some of the 276 women could become victims again."[35]

This intolerable status quo must be challenged and must be changed.

Samuel Ajayi Crowther was living proof that revolutionary change is possible when he told the Queen of England during their 1851 meeting in Windsor Castle that slavery would end if its supporters were deposed. That message prompted the secretary of state for foreign affairs to send a clear message to slave-trading King Kosoko: "Great Britain is a strong power . . . her friendship is worth having . . . her displeasure is well to avoid."[36]

Where are those international voices today?

Five

LAWLESS

In the same village the militants also killed a mom who was twenty-five years old. Her 3-month-old was able to survive a bullet to the head but a 6-year-old was hacked to death.
—Samuel Smith, *Christian Post*

D o you want to become like Leah Sharibu?"

That's the question Grace's Fulani captors asked when they presented their brutal ultimatum: pay or die. She would have to find someone who would pay a ransom, *immediately*, or the Fulani militants would sell her to Boko Haram—proof that the Fulanis have some link with the terrorist group.

We will always remember meeting Grace.

She told us they'd captured her around Christmas on a well-traveled road, along with other Christians excited to be reunited with loved ones for the holiday. The incident had quickly unfolded at a makeshift checkpoint set up by Fulani bandits a mile or so beyond the government checkpoint staffed by the police.

The proximity of the two checkpoints makes it next to impossible to believe that the police weren't aware the Fulani criminals were right down the road from their garrison. Why didn't they act to protect their citizens? Was someone paid off to turn a blind eye, or is this the accepted new normal in Africa's largest democracy?

Grace's captors forced the van she was riding in to the side of the road. Christian male passengers were quickly killed, and Christian women were forced into the bush while Muslims were freed. Grace explained that this selection practice is so common in today's Nigeria that many Christian women cover their heads and no longer travel with their documents that immediately identify them as Christians.

There's at least a slim chance of not being kidnapped if you're not an infidel.

Grace frustrated her captors when she initially couldn't think of anyone in her family who was capable of paying any ransom amount, let alone the sums they were demanding. Her murderous captors became more and more enraged, threatening to get their money by selling her as a slave to Boko Haram. That's when G-d reminded her of her pastor. In desperation, she wrote down his number. "Maybe my pastor will know someone," she pleaded.

It was Sunday. They dialed immediately.

When we met her pastor, sitting alongside a recently freed Grace, he told us that at first he didn't answer the number because it was unfamiliar to him and he was in the middle of his sermon.

But they called him again.

And then again.

Finally, the pastor apologized to his church members and said, "I think I must answer the call."

When he answered, the kidnappers didn't mince words. They told him who they had, what they wanted, and then they hung up.

The stunned and shaken pastor then did what you or I would do. He called the police, giving them the telephone numbers for Grace and her kidnappers, and he waited for something to happen—some guidance, some intervention, anything.

But the only thing he received was silence.

Grace later told us that at points during her desperate ordeal, government security forces were so close to where she was being held that she could see the soldiers' faces. She was also clever enough to keep her cell phone hidden and turned on so that authorities could track and locate her if they tried. But they never did.

Grace's only tenuous lifeline was her poor village pastor, whose flock was made up of simple and poor folks. He was suddenly thrust into the role of hostage negotiator, having to deal with criminals with a short fuse who made exorbitant financial demands. The pastor's bank account was nearly empty, and the churchgoers couldn't handle the sudden, crushing demands on their own. But he knew that if he didn't find a solution quickly, Grace would be lost forever.

He told us that he prayed to G-d and then reminded himself that "she is a member of my flock, so she is my family. I have to help her." But seminary hadn't trained him to negotiate with kidnappers. While he managed to stretch out the negotiations—buying more time to somehow come up with the ransom—they became more belligerent, threatening him and threatening Grace unless he could deliver. Time was running out.

That's when the pastor decided to start selling all his worldly possessions.

Eventually he had sold virtually everything he owned, and he sold what the church owned, and—with some additional outside donors—he finally scraped together just enough money to meet the demands.

That's when he made his last call to the kidnappers. But his heart sank when they told him that he would have to make the ransom delivery himself. "Go hire a car and come with the money to the meeting point," they instructed him. The problem was that the poor pastor now didn't have any money to rent a car. He only had enough for the ransom.

They screamed at him, berated him, and again threatened him and Grace.

His heart beat through his chest.

He prayed.

Suddenly they relented. "Just take some of the money and use it to get to us," they demanded.

The pastor complied and stopped at the designated spot, alone with the cash in hand. Miraculously, the exchange followed, and his parishioner Grace, suddenly a freed Christian woman, collapsed in gratitude to G-d and her pastor for saving her life.

We were in awe of the courage of this quiet man who is

slightly built but a giant, spiritually speaking, with nerves of steel. He had no idea if he was throwing his life away in a trap to kidnap him too—or worse. Yet he knew he had to act to help this woman in need, no matter the consequences—even if he perished trying.

Throughout our meeting the pastor said little about himself. He was totally focused on and committed to those whom he believed G-d had put in his care. We learned that this quiet hero had even risked his life by traversing those same dangerous roads just to get to our clandestine meeting in Abuja. But he never hesitated. The same faith and commitment that propelled him to risk his life for Grace motivated him to meet with two Americans in the hope that they could help awaken the world's conscience to the terrible ordeals thousands like him are experiencing every single day.

He treated Grace with respect and honor in our presence. She wore her finest clothes to come see us, with her dignity entirely intact even though she still bore the face of someone climbing her way out of the depths of a clinical shock.

The pastor was dressed in the clothes of a simple workman, but he couldn't mask his uncommon strength and resolve. He was a spiritual leader with dirt underneath his fingernails and with calluses on his hands, not one who bemoaned suffering from behind the safety of the walls of his cathedral. He reminded us of the type of shepherd—to borrow from Pope Francis—who "smells like sheep."[1]

Before the pastor left, we asked him about developments at his church.

He quietly responded, "Oh, we don't have a church building anymore. It was burned in 2018. We now meet in a tent, but that's okay. The church is not the building—it's the people."

When we asked what had happened, he explained that they still didn't know exactly who burned the church down; it could have been a group of radicalized neighbors who weren't happy that Christians gathered to pray there. It was clearly arson.

"Actually," he added, "it was the second church I've had destroyed. The first was in 2012 when Boko Haram attacked our region and destroyed hundreds of churches and homes."

Perhaps it was indelicate to ask, but we had to know: "Why do you stay if you have to suffer so much?"

That's when he told us about a wonderful opportunity he had turned down a few years earlier. Many people who meet this village pastor recognize that he possesses special gifts. He not only cares well for his congregation, but he's also a great teacher. He'd been given the opportunity to leave this dangerous part of the country and to assume care of a larger congregation in a safer part of Nigeria's majority-Christian South.

He turned down the opportunity even though it meant reaching more people in a comfortable and safer setting.

"Why?" we asked, but we already knew his answer.

"How can I leave the people G-d has entrusted to me?"

Here was the embodiment of one of Judaism's most powerful teachings codified in the Talmud: "To save one life is to save the world."[2]

A KIDNAPPER'S PARADISE

Tragically, the details of Grace's harrowing experience of being kidnapped a stone's throw from government security is not unique. We met several others who described the same scenario. It seems that if you ask ten Nigerians, eight of them will tell you they've heard a similar tale, and most of them will know someone who has been in a situation that was too close for comfort.

Nigeria regularly ranks among the top ten countries in the world in number of kidnappings. It has the distinction of being the country in Africa with the most kidnappings; they are a daily occurrence in virtually every state.[3] No one is spared from the ever-present threat of extortion.

Abdulmalik Mohammed Durunguwa, a government official from Kaduna, told Al Jazeera about the time he was kidnapped from his own home. The criminals demanded that he pay them with money or his life. He managed to arrange payment after being in captivity for seven days, but the criminals additionally demanded that he pass along a message "to tell the government . . . that 'most of them are unemployed. . . . [I]f they are not employed they will keep on kidnapping people.'"[4] In the same report a Christian pastor recounted the torture he'd suffered in a forest until his family was able to pay a ransom of two hundred dollars.

Even Turkey's TRT World news network published an article stating that "Nigeria's kidnapping cartels thrive in the absence of governance."[5]

Sometimes the attacks are especially brazen, as in the case of fifty-year-old teacher Muhammed Usman. He was taking a short bus ride from the capital of Zamfara State to his family's village only fifty kilometers away.

Suddenly a gang with advanced weapons opened fire on the bus, simultaneously attacking it from the front and the back. Usman happened to be sitting with a small child whom he instinctively covered, only to discover that he was too late. A bullet had struck the child's head, killing him instantly.

Usman was the lone survivor of the attack. He was taken hours away, deep into a forest, where he was chained in a small hut while his kidnappers attempted to find someone who would agree to pay them for his release. They constantly threatened to kill him.[6]

He made it out alive but barely.

Philip Ataga's wife, Bola, didn't.

Philip was a doctor in Kaduna, and he had become more and more worried about the kidnappings in the area, so he decided to do something about it. He donated a police station to his local community. It was "located barely 50 meters from his home."[7]

In February 2020, two weeks before our visit to Nigeria, Philip's home was besieged by a group of Fulani militants. The ordeal lasted three hours, and every effort "made to reach the police and military high authorities" fifty meters away failed.[8]

When the criminals finally retreated, they did so with Philip's wife and children in their vehicles. After seven days of extortion, it became clear that Philip couldn't pay the $380,000 they were demanding for his wife, so they killed her and "dumped her corpse and called her husband and directed him to pick [up] the corpse at a particular location."[9]

When Nigeria's news network TheCable heard of the tragedy, they immediately contacted the local police, who seemed entirely oblivious, saying that they were "not aware" that Bola had been killed. "I have not received such information," a spokesperson told the paper, "but I will find out from the officers handling the investigations and get back."[10]

But he never did "get back" to the paper. Then the kidnappers, without missing a beat, demanded $50,000 for the release of Philip's children, who were eventually freed.[11]

These terrorist maniacs, in April 2020, even attacked a wedding in progress. An eyewitness recounted the moment, saying that "as the pastor was officiating [the wedding], the herdsmen stormed the church and took away everyone who was unable to escape from the church building, including the bride and groom."[12]

Within days, Fulani militants also kidnapped a church elder in the neighboring state. "After shooting into the air to send villagers scampering into the bushes, the herdsmen broke into [Emmanuel Iliya Agiya]'s home," and they "took him away at gunpoint."[13] He was the son of the Christian village's chief.

The attacks are so frequent and so similar that it's hard to keep track of them all. While we were collaborating on this very chapter, another outrage was reported, where more than twenty people were killed in the state of Kaduna. A local press statement reported that "they broke into the home of Jonathan Yakubu, 40, and slaughtered him. They also killed his wife, Sheba Yakubu, 32, and hacked to death their only three children."[14] Their children were thirteen, six, and four years old. Their names were Patience, Revelation, and Rejoice.

In the same village, the militants also killed a mom who was twenty-five years old. "Her 3-month-old was able to survive a bullet to the head but a 6-year-old was hacked to death. . . . Others killed in the attack on the home also include[d] 32-year-old Asanalo Magaji and 13-year-old Yayo Magaji."[15] The names and ages continue in the reporting: a six-month-old baby, a couple in their twenties, a sixty-year-old who nearly escaped, a husband and wife with their fourteen-year-old granddaughter, whose name was Blessing.

Then there were two attacks on other villages not far away. There the militants killed a father of seven, a man who was eighty, another who was seventy, another who was forty, and one who was forty-five. Then there was a thirty-seven-year-old. . . . The silent cries of the victims seem to scream out from this endless list of horrors. With all the savagery, one other recent attack demands our attention.

It was about six o'clock one evening in April 2020, when the Fulani militants arrived in Ezekiel Isa's Christian village. There were about 160 of them—a small army with military-grade weapons. The attackers were all Muslims. They were shouting "Allahu Akbar," when they arrived, according to what Isa, a twenty-seven-year-old local, told the press. "They were speaking Fulani language, which we don't know, but we could understand [some of] their words in our Hausa language, and they were saying 'kill 150, kill 150, they are infidels, kill them!'"[16]

Isa then said, "This is not the first time we faced attacks by the Fulani terrorists. They had killed many of our village last year."[17] In this new attack, which lasted about two hours, the terrorists burned to the ground more than fifty homes and displaced six hundred members of the community.

This time, though, the terrorists inadvertently left behind evidence: a cell phone was found "amid butchered bodies and scattered wreckage," and in this case, it "was not password-protected."[18]

According to the reporter recounting the tragedy of Isa's village, it isn't uncommon for this type of forensic evidence to be found, because "cell phones have been found in the wake of previous attacks. A cell phone was recovered at an Irigwe village massacre in Plateau State in 2018 and was turned over to police. No arrests or prosecution followed."[19]

Why is this powerful evidence not used by the Nigerian authorities to track and prosecute these perpetrators before they raze another village and chop to pieces more babies? With nobody trying to find them, these crazed murderers are emboldened and empowered to systematically execute the innocent with total impunity again and again.

A senior government official in one of the states most affected by these raids wrote these salient words in a private memo we were able to review:

> [The] very lackadaisical attitude of the Federal government
> gives the herdsmen the impression that they are being protected
> by the corridors of power in Nigeria and also [allows them to]

freely move about with dangerous weapons unchecked. . . . [I]
n addition, the inability of the Federal Government to take
cogent steps to punish the perpetrators of this mayhem across
the country to serve as a deterrent to others further emboldens
the herdsmen and weakens the bond in nationhood.[20]

When the state of Benue—sometimes called the food bas-
ket of Nigeria—decided to take real action by enacting a law to
protect farmers through limiting open grazing by herdsmen,
it ignited armed attacks by certain groups of Fulani herdsmen
largely believed to be provoked by the more mainstream Miyetti
Allah Cattle Breeders Association of Nigeria (MACBAN).

As tensions increased and armed resistance to the law continued, the governor of Benue State wrote multiple letters to the
federal government appealing for help, letters we've reviewed.
He wrote to the inspector general of the police, saying that he
would like to draw the inspector's "attention to the imminent
threat by the leadership of Miyetti Allah Kautal Hore. . . . Benue
has experienced the influx of armed herdsmen, who have violently and systematically attacked many communities in the
State."[21]

In his letter to the vice president, one official cited statistics quantifying the attacks, saying that "over 99,427 households
were affected in Benue State and property worth billions of Naira
destroyed."[22] President Buhari was warned about "alleged armed
Fulani militia buildup and convergence at the Nigeria-Cameroon
border and at the Agatu border with Nasarawa State to the North-
West of Benue State." The leader for a delegation of socio-cultural

groups in Benue stated, "It is being reliably gathered that leaders of the herdsmen have held clandestine meetings in Nigeria and abroad to visit mayhem and genocide on the people of Benue State."[23]

The federal government's response was—and remains—dismal.

Eventually a private organization filed a lawsuit against the federal government for violating the human rights of Benue State's residents. The federal government argued in court that the violence wasn't their responsibility because "what was happening in Benue State was communal clashes between farmers and herders."[24]

The federal government lost the case in March 2019, with the court ordering the immediate creation of an independent commission to study the atrocities committed by Fulani herdsmen and to deploy security to the area.

This week alone, while we have been writing this chapter, multiple attacks have occurred in Benue State, and there is little sign of any change in attitude or action by the nation's leaders.

When you ask affected Nigerians why the government doesn't do more, they often reference President Buhari's own lifelong membership in MACBAN and that organization's support of Buhari as a fellow Fulani.

During Buhari's recent election campaign, the leaders of MACBAN traveled to his villa to tender their endorsement. When they did, to his credit, Buhari declared, "I appeal to all farmers and herders for restraint, mutual respect and tolerance for one another as people destined to live together in this great country. I appeal for patience and understanding as the administration works towards lasting solutions to these conflicts."[25]

It was an important gesture, yet one might think from reading it that these groups are attacking one another. On the contrary, with few exceptions, this is a war of an aggressor and its victim.

In 2019, the Christian Association of Nigeria (CAN) called upon President Buhari to cancel his MACBAN membership and to issue an outright ban of the organization because of its alleged support of kidnapping, extortion, and the destruction of villages. The CAN spokesman added that Buhari should also "immediately disarm and prosecute the Fulani herdsmen terrorists."[26]

There was no action and no response—just more violence. Which once again begs the question: Does anyone care about these beautiful, innocent lives? And where is the government?

Here's one clue: it lies within the cell phone left behind in the ruins of an attacked village, the one the authorities haven't examined. Maybe they haven't because among the saved contact information are the phone numbers of numerous members of Nigeria's army and police officers.

Six

DOWN BUT NOT OUT

If you say, "But we knew nothing about this,"
does not he who weighs the heart perceive it?
Does not he who guards your life know it?
—PROVERBS 24:12

errorists had already released a videotape of the beheading
of eleven Nigerian Christians on Christmas Day 2019,[1] when
twenty-two-year-old Ropvil Daciya Dalep was kidnapped a mere
two weeks later.

Ropvil, a student majoring in biology at the University of
Maiduguri, was abducted just outside of the capital of Borno
State as he traveled back to school following a festive Christmas
holiday with family and friends.[2] He would never be seen again
except on a video released by the Boko Haram offshoot called
ISIS in the West Africa Province (ISWAP).

In the video, Ropvil was on his knees in an orange jumpsuit

reminiscent of ISIS executions in Iraq and Syria. Standing behind Ropvil was a masked terrorist clad in black with a handgun in his right hand. The terrorist then began to speak of Ropvil as "one among the Christians from Plateau State. We are saying to Christians, we have not forgotten what you have done to our parents and ancestors and we are telling all Christians around the world, we have not forgotten and will not stop. We must avenge the bloodshed that has been done, like this one."[3]

Then the terrorist raised his pistol and executed Ropvil at point-blank range. Ropvil was twenty-two. The terrorist was probably no older than twelve.

The child beneath the mask had been brainwashed into becoming a murderer, with his cowardly handlers celebrating their theft of this youngster's innocence. They had adopted the tactics honed by ISIS in Iraq and Syria when it came to abducting children, which were detailed in *Defying ISIS*:

> There are as many horrifying stories as there are children whom ISIS has encountered. In the Syrian city of Kobani, they abducted more than 150 Kurdish boys between the ages of fourteen and sixteen, beating them ruthlessly with hoses and electric cables.
>
> They forced them to memorize misinterpreted religious sayings. If they weren't able to perfectly recite them they were beaten more. One of the boys who escaped said they asked them for addresses of family members so that they might "get them and cut them up."
>
> In the Syrian city of Raqqa, the "capital of the Islamic

State," children were forcibly enrolled in ISIS-controlled "training camps" where they were taught how to decapitate people. One of those was a thirteen-year-old boy named Mohammad. His mother explained,

> After his return [from camp] his mother says she was surprised to find in his bag a blond, blue-eyed doll—along with a large knife given to her son by his ISIS supervisors. When she confronted Mohammad, he told her that the camp manager had distributed the dolls and asked that the children decapitate them using the knife, and that they were asked to cover the dolls' faces when they performed the decapitation. It was his homework: practice beheading a toy likeness of a blond, white Westerner.

Brainwashed children have been forced to join the ISIS army as "Cubs of the Islamic State," and "instead of archery and merit badges . . . these boys learn how to clean, dissemble, and shoot machine guns. . . . They make them watch a beheading, and sometimes they force them to carry the heads in order to cast the fear away from their hearts." Child soldiers are sometimes used as human shields or are forced to become suicide bombers. In a little-publicized video from a playground in Syria, an ISIS teacher is recorded threatening to kill the children if they don't comply. He says he will cut them as they slaughter sheep.

In a much more publicized video, a "Cub of the Islamic State"—probably twelve years old—shoots two ISIS prisoners in the head at point-blank range. The child has a stoic look on his face, already drained of his natural human proclivities and manipulated into becoming a murderer. He has long dark hair and eyes that are as black as night. He strikes terror in you as you look at him there with his ISIS overlord looking approvingly on as he executes those who have chosen not to believe.

The stories go on and on.

The United Nations Human Rights Commission "has received numerous reports" citing the recruitment of children as young as thirteen to fight alongside ISIS. A UN report states, "Witnesses claimed that the majority of ISIL elements patrolling the streets of Mosul were underage children, aged 13 to 16 years." Children have been seen wearing masks over their faces and carrying guns almost as large as their bodies.

Children robbed of their innocence and forced to kill.[4]

This wasn't the first time that Nigeria's terrorists deployed the tactics of ISIS after the group's near-total demise in Iraq and Syria. There are countless examples, but one that caught the attention of virtually everyone in Nigeria (and too few people elsewhere) was the September 2019 case of Lawrence Duna Dacighir and Godfrey Ali Shikagham.

The video of their execution was temporarily on YouTube, but before its removal, it spread throughout the country via other social networks. Once again in orange jumpsuits, the two men were on their knees when their executioners said, "[This is the beginning of] revenge on Christians in Plateau State."[5] Then they were shot from behind by masked killers.

Lawrence and Godfrey, who had been members of the Church of Christ in Nigeria, had been traveling to Maiduguri "to help build shelters for people displaced by Islamic extremist violence."[6] Pastor John Pofi, cousin to these two men, recalled that they had left "in search of opportunities to utilize their skills for the betterment of humanity and paid with their lives."[7]

Just one week before the public execution of Lawrence and Godfrey, there had been another widely publicized attack in Kaduna State—this time by Fulani militants. They targeted an evangelical church in Birnin Gwari. The attack began near midnight, and the town's pastor, Rev. Ishaku Katung, was injured in the attack while his wife, Esther, was kidnapped.[8]

The Fulani raiders immediately demanded a ransom of $13,000 for her release. That was an impossible sum for the pastor, but he negotiated until they were willing to accept just over $1,100. He paid the ransom but never saw his pregnant wife again. He later learned from others who were released that she "had died after suffering a severe beating the day before the ransom was received."[9]

Mervyn Thomas, the CEO of Christian Solidarity Worldwide in the United Kingdom, declared, "Given that the Nigerian constitution asserts that the 'security and welfare of the people' are the 'primary purpose of government,' we urge the authorities to do everything in their power to safeguard citizens and bring perpetrators to justice."[10]

In a news report an enraged secretary general of CAN for Kaduna State bemoaned that human life no longer means anything in the country. The reporter sought a comment on the murder of Esther Katung from the Kaduna State Police Command's public relations officer but "was unsuccessful as his mobile phone was switched off."[11]

Clearly, the government cell phones aren't accepting incoming calls or have blocked cries for justice. Nigeria's leaders are either uninterested in the fate of citizens targeted by terrorists or incapable of doing anything about it.

In that same month when Esther, Lawrence, and Godfrey were butchered, the huge aid agency Mercy Corps announced it was leaving two states in northeastern Nigeria after the Nigerian Army "closed four of its offices in the region."[12] Without any protection for their activities, they had to leave 150,000 displaced people without desperately needed humanitarian help.[13]

Perhaps more embarrassed by closing the offices of aid agencies than by the murders of its citizens, the Nigerian Army deflected questions by accusing Mercy Corps of helping the terrorists! No evidence was ever produced to back up this slanderous attack. One official speculated that the actual reason for closing the offices was to stop reports that helped create the bad public relations the country was receiving because of the escalating humanitarian crisis.[14]

At the same time, Nigerian authorities were busy negotiating with the terrorists. It is interesting to note that along with the graphic video of the murders of Lawrence and Godfrey came the executioners' reasons for killing the Christian men: "because 'the government deceived them' following months of what is now known as secret negotiations between a team of intermediaries and unnamed officials."[15]

Meanwhile, the executioners' comments about the Christians in Plateau State, as well as those of the boy who killed Ropvil, represent corroborating evidence that there is some link between Fulani militants in the middle of the country and the Boko Haram and ISIS terrorists in the Northeast.

Just stop and think about that. Here are armed insurgents behaving as ISIS did in Iraq and Syria, massacring aid workers and women. They are razing entire villages, kidnapping people, chopping children into pieces, and threatening Nigeria's president by name. They are engaging in all kinds of criminal activities in an attempt to ethnically cleanse Nigeria of its vulnerable northern Christians. Along the way they are also threatening and sometimes massacring any Muslim who attempts to stand in their way—and there are many who oppose them.

All of this is destabilizing Africa's largest country, home to the continent's biggest economy. Nigeria is also a recipient of at least $1 billion in aid annually from the United States and more than 800,000 pounds daily in aid from the United Kingdom.

And has the government moved to crush these terrorists? No, they pay their ransoms and then negotiate with them through intermediaries who clearly know where the terrorists are and what they are demanding.

Lawrence and Godfrey's cousin, Pastor Pofi, clearly stated that "we must ask ourselves if this is the kind of country we want where young men who are earning an honest living are brutally killed while those who abduct and kill others are invited to dialogue with [the] government and paid handsomely."[16]

IS IT ANY WONDER THEY KILLED THE CHAIRMAN?

On January 2, 2020, Boko Haram had taken Lawan Andimi, the chairman of CAN in Adamawa State. Then they made the pastor record a video to his community as proof of life.

We'll never forget the near supernatural peace and strength evident in the composed and fearless words of this senior religious leader. His was a haunting, unfathomable courage! Wearing a track sweater zipped up, he sat on the floor in front of a yellow tent or wall. Just behind his left shoulder was draped the infamous black flag of ISIS, which has been adopted by Boko Haram since 2015.

The demeanor accompanying his words was itself in defiance of that black ISIS flag. Terrorists aim to cause *terror* in their victims, but they clearly failed in causing Andimi to fear them at all. To the contrary, his strength revealed their cowardice.

He seemed to embody the words of Psalm 23:4—a passage the Jewish sage Rashi says David wrote while contemplating his closest encounter with death:

> Even though I walk
>> through the darkest valley,
> I will fear no evil,
>> for *you* are with me" (emphasis ours).

Andimi said in the video, "I have never been discouraged, because all conditions that one finds himself [in] . . . [are] in the hand of G-d."[17] Then Pastor Andimi did what the terrorists, no doubt, asked him to do: "I am appealing to my colleagues, reverends, particularly my president, Reverend Joel Billi, who is a strong man, a man of compassion and man of love. He can do all his best to speak to our governor . . . and other necessary agents for my release here."[18]

He also stated his hope that "he might return to his family and colleagues 'by the grace of G-d. . . . If the opportunity has not been granted, maybe it is the will of G-d. . . . Don't cry, don't worry, but thank G-d for everything."[19]

On January 21, Pastor Andimi was beheaded for his faith after "the church did everything within her reach to secure the safe release of this pastor gentlemen," the legal and public affairs director of CAN told the press.[20]

Pastor Andimi's widow was in Abuja visiting with local Christian leaders during our visit to the city. On the second anniversary of Leah Sharibu's kidnapping, Pastor Andimi's widow appeared at a press conference with Dr. Paul Enenche, the founder of one of the world's largest evangelical churches, whose building—called Dunamis Glory Dome—sits on the road between the airport and Abuja.

Mrs. Andimi, with one of her nine children sitting behind her, began her testimony by saying, "Hallelujah and Amen"— hardly words either of us would have the strength to utter if one of our loved ones had received the treatment those terrorists had given to her husband.

She reflected on the peace in their home immediately before the incident, saying that "we were home eating, having fun with the whole family." That's when someone came to their door and warned them that Boko Haram was on its way to their village.

They took two different routes to get out of Dodge. Mrs. Andimi and their children "ran away to the hills" while Pastor Andimi—always a leader—found a car to get others out of the village. But in every direction they drove, they kept finding there was no escape route. Someone told Pastor Andimi of another way out, but it proved to be unsafe. This happened again and again until they eventually came to the main road—the main thoroughfare to the city, because surely the terrorists weren't so brazen—only to find that the terrorists were traveling on that main road themselves in broad daylight. Pastor Andimi immediately took another road, only to discover there were attackers there too.

That's when they took him.

Initially, Mrs. Andimi didn't know they had taken her husband. When she returned to the village with their children, at first she was encouraged because their village had been spared. But when she began searching everywhere for her husband, she became worried and started to cry.

A hush fell over the crowd of Dr. Enenche's massive church as she told of asking one of those in the village, "Where is Daddy?" In Nigeria, as in other parts of Africa, *daddy* is a term of endearment used not only within one's family but within a community, especially for a respected spiritual leader.

Her neighbor replied, "They [meaning others in the village] took Daddy with them when they escaped."

In her local language of Hausa, Mrs. Andimi said, "In that moment, I felt in my spirit that something was wrong with my husband."

The next time she saw him was in the video the terrorists sent in conjunction with a demand that CAN pay hundreds of thousands of dollars or they would kill Andimi. The ransom amount seems extraordinary in a deeply impoverished place, but the government's willingness to pay millions in recent years may have increased the value of all those captured. This is why the United States has a long-standing policy of never paying ransom for hostages.

The whole community began to fast and pray for their beloved pastor, and then the good news came. The head of their church denomination came to tell Mrs. Andimi that "by the grace of G-d, your husband will be released. We were able to find just over one hundred thousand dollars, and the terrorists have agreed to release him."

She said, "Everyone was jubilant. I immediately went home and informed the children that their daddy would be coming home."

It was only the next day when Mrs. Andimi was approached by the leaders of the church denomination. She ran to them with joy. "Have you concluded the negotiation? When will he be home?"

They calmly asked her to sit down, as one of them withdrew a phone from his pocket. The next thing she would see was the video of her husband's grotesque murder. Not a government official or police officer in sight. The church was left to disclose the tragedy, to negotiate with the terrorists, and to somehow protect the vulnerable from the next attack.

And how did Mrs. Andimi respond to the horrifying video?

Of course she wilted in sorrow, but then—moments after learning in such a painful way that she was now a widow, left to raise their nine children—she remembered what her husband had said on the previous video sent by the terrorists. He encouraged her to take care of the children, and that no matter what happened, her faith should be strong. And she remembered her husband's words, "Don't cry, don't worry."

Sharing her story with the church congregation as well as the nation through the national press listening in, she said, "I thanked G-d that my husband did not denounce his faith." She mentioned that walking into Dr. Enenche's church that day brought a serenity to her. It brought her peace. She looked at the camera in front of her and said, "Our area is full of these incidents [of violence and terror]; let's keep praying for Christians in vulnerable parts of Nigeria."

That's when her son, who looks just like his father, asked for the microphone. "Praise the Lord. Our daddy used to advise us and encourage us to stand firm in our faith no matter what happened."[21]

Stand firm. They have.

But no one in Nigeria—or the world—ought to need this much faith just to live another day. Dr. Enenche pledged then and there to cover all the expenses for the future of Mrs. Andimi's children.

THE TERRORISTS LIVE

While virtually everyone seems to think the horror of ISIS has been relegated to the dustbin of evildoers of history, we clearly saw that ISIS has simply migrated to a different part of the world.

What's happening in Nigeria is the latest mutation of the long tale of modern Islamist extremism from Sayyid Qutb to Ayman al-Zawahiri to Osama bin Laden to Abu Musab al-Zarqawi to Abu Bakr al-Baghdadi to the leaders of Boko Haram.

Its epicenter has traveled from Saudi Arabia and Egypt to Sudan and then to Somalia and then to Afghanistan. The epicenter shifted to Iraq and Syria, and now it is shifting to the northeast of Nigeria. It is present in countless countries and in the hearts of millions of potential lone-wolf extremists throughout the entire world. But always there have been epicenters serving as Terrorism Central.

One of those epicenters is within the country with more Christians than any other on the continent, a country that represents a dividing line between its Islamic North and its Christian South, a country rich with oil and poor in governance, a country where horror and terror are allowed to roam freely with no accountability. As Isaiah 59:15 says, "Truth is nowhere to be found, / and whoever shuns evil becomes a prey. / The LORD looked and was displeased / that there was no justice."

The time has more than come to rescue those being led away to death:

Rescue those being led away to death;

hold back those staggering toward slaughter.

If you say, "But we knew nothing about this,"

does not he who weighs the heart perceive it?

Does not he who guards your life know it?

Will he not repay everyone according to what they have
done? (Proverbs 24:11–12)

seven

THOUSANDS OF NAMES

*This issue of COVID-19, we don't know
anything about it, but our problem
is Fulani who are killing us!*
—PASTOR YAKUBU KPASHA

As activists struggle to find the right key to awaken the world's conscience to the perilous situation unfolding in Nigeria, it is important to remember that this crisis isn't new. The world has turned a blind eye for at least a decade. Some have defaulted to a willful ignorance while others have found solace in raging indifference.

The expanding deadly midnight raids, arsons, kidnappings, rapes, forced conversions, steady and pernicious ethnic cleansing, and silent cries of tens of thousands of innocents fall on deaf ears. And all the events in recent years have unfolded before our eyes in the information age, in the era of YouTube and tweets. All of it is taking place in a modern democracy that communicates in English with a local press, often reporting on the unspeakable atrocities in real time. Survivors of earlier mayhem and the families whose loved ones have been butchered have every right to indict an uncaring world whose inaction confirms that their loved ones' suffering and martyrdom may have been in vain and, worse, totally forgotten!

So at least here on these pages, in this modest narrative, we remember those who died or barely survived the 2010 Christmas Eve attack in Jos, Nigeria. Jos serves as the center of northern Christianity with a Catholic archdiocese, a local Anglican diocese, and an Anglican archdiocese for the province of Jos. It is also the headquarters to numerous denominations, seminaries, and mission societies.

There have been many, many attacks in Jos, but the Christmas Eve bombing signaled that a new redline had been breached. More than a decade later, it is clear the brazenness of that assault should have served as an early warning sign. When it began around seven that evening, this is what people experienced: "A transit bus bursts into flames, streaking the night sky with orange and red. Burning shops, homes and automobiles add an eerie, dancing light. Building walls are sprayed with black film. The smell of chemicals, heat, and charred wood permeate the air."[1]

A few moments later several churches were attacked, and—in the end—there would be more than eighty—*eighty!*—Christian funerals. One victim described that terrifying moment:

I was on my way back when a bomb went off near a bridge.
I had stopped to buy spices so I could cook. The bomb went

off, and I was lifted off the ground. When I fell down, I tried to stand up. But I fell down again, and I realized my leg had been blown off.

After the accident, I was taken to the hospital, and my leg had to be amputated. Now I walk slowly. I fall down. I don't even know who paid for my medical bills. It might have been the government, but I don't know for sure.

My church has been helpful. I have five children, and they support me as well. I live with my daughter and her husband. I am following the Lord strongly because he spared me. Many died that day, so I have a lot that I owe him. I always thank him. Since he spared me, it means he wants me to carry on his work.[2]

Here's another eyewitness account:

I am a worker and have two children. My mom has her own fabric shop in a market.

On Christmas Eve, I took off work to help her at her shop because she had lots of customers coming. I noticed Muslims came and left something nearby. But I didn't pay attention, because I was busy. Around 7:00 p.m., the bomb blew up in the shop.

It killed many people. That's how I got this injury on my leg. I was rushed to a nearby hospital, where they started treatment. There were not enough doctors to treat me. I had my leg amputated and now have an artificial limb.

Now, I've been buying medicine day in and day out. I cannot work at my old job.

My mother is aging. Her business has collapsed. She is depressed. I can't work enough, and I can't care for her. My children are still small. They look up to me. But I cannot even pick them up because I can't lift heavy things now. My injuries handicap me. My mother depends on me. She needs me to help care for her financially. But I depend on others to give me simple jobs. I have to care for my wife and children, too, so I need consistent work.

I'm telling you, this is real life for us. It's only through the help of G-d that we have survived. . . . Without him we can do nothing.[3]

And still the list of victims grows and grows. Hundreds of churches have been attacked, and millions of people have been directly affected in various ways.

In one state alone, a partial list of churches attacked by Fulani militants included these:

The Catholic Church Bunzung	LCCN Bujun
	ECWA Wagure
LCCN Baffa	Catholic Church Bujun
UMC Bujun Yashi	Waya
LCCN Sakpani	ECWA Bujun Yashi
UMC Kuruke	UMC Kpantilade
ECWA Bujun Kasuwa	ECWA Yitti
Deeper Life Bunzung	UMC Todung
UMC Kashedi	Anglican Church Bantaji
LCCN Bujun Waya	St. Philips Vicarage Ibi

St. James Anglican Church

St. Andrew's Church

Dan Anacha

Chinkai

St. Philips School Ibi

St. James Anglican Church

St. Paul's Church Chediya

Dan Anacha

St. Thomas Anglican
Church Sai Dampar

Epiphany Church Tella

We reviewed a list of nearly one hundred villages attacked in another state from 2015 to 2018. Each attack wreaked havoc on the lives and livelihood of innocent Nigerians, crippling infrastructure and destroying any hope for the future. Take, for instance, one assault that took place on December 26, 2017, resulting in "a colossal loss of lives . . . 306 round huts [and] 5 zinc houses razed, assorted grains burnt to ashes, [and] church instruments destroyed, [as well as] milling machines, two motorcycles, two grinding machines, a wheel barrow, a sewing machine, [and] generators were burnt . . . *entire . . . communities were displaced*"[4] (emphasis ours).

In another town, where eighty-six people, including three pastors, had been killed a year earlier, eleven churches were destroyed and thousands of animals killed or stolen.[5]

Consider for a few moments the fate of a single group— the Irigwe people. According to the International Committee on Nigeria, there are about a hundred thousand of them in the country. They are mainly Christian and live almost entirely in the state of Plateau.[6]

One report cited that between September 2017 and July 2019, sixty-six attacks across more than fifty villages displaced at least fifteen thousand individuals, leaving nearly *two hundred widows* and nearly *eight hundred orphans* in their wake. Thousands of small farms were destroyed. When the police were contacted for comment by Nigeria's *Daily Post*, the spokesperson said "the police were working with 'neighborhood watch' to ensure security for communities affected."[7]

In spite of the announced inadequate steps to protect the people, attacks have continued unabated against this group in 2020, even in the middle of the COVID-19 pandemic. Abbah Yoki told a Nigerian news outlet that "he was the Black-clad attackers' first target as he left his room at about 7 a.m. . . . [when] he saw 10 Fulani tribesmen split into three groups." He was shot in the leg, but they killed his two children, his neighbor, and his pastor.[8]

In a dramatic interview with the press, as another local evangelical pastor was "putting his hand on the wall of a burned out school," he said that "this issue of COVID-19, we don't know anything about it, but our problem is Fulani who are killing us!"[9] He then listed those who were killed in his congregation and noted that it was also the second time he had a church destroyed.

The sheer scale of this man-made crisis is mind-boggling. It just goes on and on and on. Calculated attacks are countless. If we were to detail all of them, in their blood- and tear-soaked entirety, this book would be thousands of pages long.

You get the point. Or do you?

In a private letter to human rights activists, the immediate previous Anglican archbishop of Jos, the Most Rev. Ben Kwashi, put it bluntly:

Until the truth is told and until justice is done, the poor in this country, and especially the poor Christians, are going to be slaughtered every day. . . . It is a common development and an everyday occurrence across Nigeria to kill Christians, meanwhile offenders are not being prosecuted and the leaders are unresponsive. Houses are destroyed, churches are ruined, schools are rendered useless, and no arrests are made.[10]

The situation is now so perilous that the United Kingdom's fierce and legendary advocate for religious freedom, Baroness Caroline Cox, has uttered the *G* word in an indictment titled "UK Government 'Turning a Deaf Ear' to Genocide in Nigeria."[11]

Baroness Cox is fully informed about the nuances that make up today's Nigeria. In fact, in a letter she wrote to the leaders of the International Organization for Peace Building and Social Justice, she said that she was urging action precisely because she understands the complexities of the issue.

While the underlying causes of violence are complex, the asymmetry and escalation of attacks by well-armed Fulani militia upon predominantly Christian communities is stark and must be acknowledged. . . . [These] attacks have, on occasion, led to retaliatory violence, as communities conclude that they can no longer rely on the Government for protection or justice. However, we have seen no evidence of comparability of scale or equivalence of atrocities. . . . [W]hile the Nigerian administration has taken steps to counter

Boko Haram insurgency it has not demonstrated the same commitment to tackle the escalating violence perpetrated by Fulani militants.[12]

She is right.

All this reminds us of the aftermath of the terrible genocide in Rwanda in 1994, which the world ignored until it was too late. Four years later, in 1998, in the aftermath of nearly one million deaths, President Clinton traveled to Kigali to apologize. "All over the world there were people like me sitting in offices, day after day after day, who did not fully appreciate the depth and the speed with which you were being engulfed by this unimaginable terror," he said. "Never again must we be shy in the face of the evidence."[13]

Today it isn't the speed of the mass murder but the crushing indifference to it that feeds the evil beast. Memory itself is under assault. Let us at least commit to remember one victim, one community, one house of worship.

A Jewish saying reminds us of what is at stake: "In remembrance lies the roots of redemption, in forgetfulness the roots of destruction."[14]

SHE WAS THIRTEEN, AND SHE CAME BACK PREGNANT

Remember Ese Oruru. It was 2015, and she was thirteen years old when she was kidnapped from her family store in Nigeria's Bayelsa State. As is the case with child trafficking, you'd expect her abduction and its aftermath to continue in the shadows, hidden from the prying eyes of strangers and far removed from the authorities.

Except that Ese was taken by her abductor directly to the palace of the emir of Kano, Sanusi Lamido Sanusi, who happened to be a former governor of the Central Bank of Nigeria[15] and remains until this day an influential figure. In March 2020, he was successfully deposed as the emir, allegedly with Buhari's blessing, only to return to his family in Lagos, where people immediately began to speak of him as a future Nigerian president.[16]

Young Ese's case captured the attention of Nigeria. The emir said publicly that when the young girl was brought to his attention by his associates in the palace the day after she arrived,[17] he "ordered her immediate repatriation to her parents" through the Kano State Sharia Commission because "nowhere in Islam [can] . . . such young girls . . . just make up their mind and give their hands in marriage just like that. It is not permitted in Islam."[18]

The right words were uttered, but Ese's reality told a different story.

By the time Ese was finally returned to her parents the following year after a public outcry, she somehow had been converted to Islam. Her name had been changed to an Islamic name, Aisha, and she was five months pregnant.[19] The young girl arrived home in a hijab.

The general secretary of CAN, Rev. Musa Asake, was enraged:

Our Christian girls are abducted but nothing is done about it. It is so sad that while we are praying to live in peace, another side is not showing a sign of peace. I don't know where it is in the religion that teaches that they can take someone's daughter, convert her from Christianity to Islam and marry her (off). If that is religion, then it is very unfortunate. I also want to make it very clear: If it were Christians doing this to Muslim girls, Nigerians would have been burnt to ashes.[20]

Reverend Asake was deferential to the emir, saying, "If his version of what transpired is true, then he doesn't need to apologize to anybody because he did speak up to say the girl should be released," but he demanded, "[the abductor] must be thrown into prison, never to see the light of day."[21]

While the abductor, Yunusa Dahiru, was arrested and tried, the process "dragged on endlessly in court,"[22] and at one point the criminal was released only to be put back in prison after missing multiple court appointments. Only now, two days after writing this chapter, was Dahiru finally convicted of his crime. The Federal High Court in Yenagoa sentenced him to twenty-six years in prison.[23] Even so, two days after the sentencing, someone sent a tweet to President Buhari's assistant for New Media, which read, "Please Bashir do something about Yunusa Yellow [referring to Ese's kidnapper] for Allah's sake, he is wrongly accused and sentenced, the whole matter is manipulated, we need to appeal for him." Bashir Ahmed replied in Hausa, "I do not have the power to do anything against the judgement of the court, but I will try to contact those whom I think are capable."[24]

In the case of such a profane crime against a child, one would expect a synchronous response from the nation's political system and religious leaders. Yet that response didn't come.

Sheikh Abdur-Rahman Ahmad, the head of Ansar-ud-Deen Society of Nigeria, one of the nation's most influential and largest mainstream Islamic organizations, offered an overtly defensive and combative interview to a widely read Nigerian media outlet. Instead of condemning child marriage, he instead attacked the theological legitimacy of the perpetrator's marriage according to Sharia law because Ese hadn't consented nor had her parents, no dowry had been paid, and there were no eyewitnesses.[25]

Instead of clearly condemning the perpetrator, who had already confessed to his crime, Ahmad said that "until we verify the claims independently, we take them as allegations which have not been proved. So I hold [the perpetrator] innocent because I have not had the opportunity to hear from him."[26]

Rather than directly condemning the criminal and his crime against a child, this leader hid behind theological technicalities. Never even uttering Ese's name, he had no words of consolation to a devastated child, family, and community.

The only interest here was in defending Islam and providing a less-than-veiled condemnation of the country's Christians for "politicizing the situation," while decrying Islamophobia in his very first comment: "It is unfortunate and it is callous of those who are holding a religion of almost two billion people responsible for the action of an individual. . . . Adolf Hitler was a Christian, has anybody blamed Christianity for his actions? I do believe it is a smokescreen; the real agenda is that this is a campaign of hate against a region [the North of Nigeria] and against a religion [Islam]."[27]

When asked later about Boko Haram's use of Islamic rhetoric, Ahmad responded with a conspiracy theory: "I do not hold Christianity responsible, [but] a lot of Boko Haram members, who were captured, were said to be Christians. Those of them who are not Christians, the media reported, that they did not even find Qurans with them . . . and Boko Haram operates in an area dominated by Muslims, so the majority of those who suffer are Muslims [anyway]."[28]His response is essentially an anti-Christian variation of a common anti-Semitic trope among Islamic extremists, who often accused Jews of orchestrating the very terror targeting them. This dangerous speech doesn't only happen overseas. A Shi'ite imam, Sayed Moustafa al-Qazwini, said as much in a 2017 sermon delivered not far from the Simon Wiesenthal Center in California:

All of you know who established ISIS, Al-Qaeda, and all of these terrorist organizations. You know very well. You know who paid for them, who financed them, who helped them, who purchased weapons for them, who even trained them, who protected them. You know that. This is not the production of Islam. Islam is not responsible for ISIS. There are certain agencies and governments, who . . . put hand in hand to establish ISIS, to demolish Islam from within. This was the plan. . . . We knew the story from the beginning. When ISIS occupied Mosul three years ago, I gave a speech in Iraq. I said: "ISIS is the production of the Israeli intelligence."[29]

During our own visit to Nigeria, we met with a respected mainstream Islamic figure who leads an organization representing millions. We had a wonderful conversation that centered around Islamic victims of terror, efforts at interfaith harmony, and the solutions required to address the conditions underlying Nigeria's conflict. Our meeting was good and meaningful. It left us hopeful.

Then, as we were accompanying the group to their vehicle, this Islamic leader leaned into us, clearly feeling comfortable and at ease, and said, "You know there were no Christians in the North to begin with. These Christians are all the product of colonialism."

His words shocked us. In other words, *Christians are actually the problem. If they weren't there, there would not be a problem.*

An honest moderate or a closet extremist? You decide.

PLEASE DON'T FORGET US

The Catholic cardinal of New York, Cardinal Timothy Dolan, wrote in 2015 about a conversation he had with the Catholic archbishop of Jos, Ignatius Kaigama, in the aftermath of the brutal terrorist attacks in Paris on the *Charlie Hebdo* newspaper headquarters and on an adjacent Jewish deli.

Millions in France and around the world had taken to the streets in solidarity. Among those forcefully condemning these attacks were the cardinal in New York and the archbishop in Jos. They were united again, as they often were, in combating religious violence, speaking for the persecuted, and—to borrow from George Washington while speaking to a Jewish congregation in 1790—"gives to bigotry no sanction."[30]

"But," Cardinal Dolan writes of that conversation with his friend, "Archbishop Kaigama, a brave, sincere, and beloved pastor, who has seen hundreds of his churches, healthcare clinics, and schools burned to the ground, and, dreadfully worse, hundreds of his good, decent, peaceful people cut to shreds by the machetes and machine guns of the Islamic radicals of *Boko Haram*, also begged, 'But, *please don't forget us!*'" (italics appear in original).[31]

During the same week as the much-publicized Paris attacks, Boko Haram attacked and essentially wiped out the northeastern town of Baga in Nigeria, killing as many as two thousand people in a single massacre.[32]

Dolan then conveyed this salient question from Kaigama: "Where are the marchers in Europe and North America condemning the continued massacres of religious minorities, especially Christians, in Africa? Are the lives of these innocent people less worthy of respect and protection than those of white Europeans?"[33]

The archbishop conveyed to the cardinal that the issue isn't that Christians and Muslims can't coexist. They have long "work[ed] together as neighbors" in Jos, and "both groups have been slaughtered by the jihadists."[34]

The issue is that the terrorists are emboldened to continue and expand their evil, convinced that Nigeria's leaders and the leaders of the world are all too willing to forget.

Will we?

Eight

THE MORAL IMPERATIVE
TO ACT

It is not your responsibility to finish the
work, but you are not free to desist from it.
—ETHICS OF THE FATHERS 2:16

Abel was a herder tending his flock, and Cain was a farmer tilling his soil. They were, according to the Genesis narrative, humankind's first brothers—the sons of Adam and Eve. Clearly, they had lived together as a family for many years, since Cain and Abel had reached the stage of work in their own lives.

Then one day the family was ripped apart. Genesis 4 tells us that the brothers were the subject of the first crime scene in human history. One was the victim and the other was the perpetrator—and these were brothers. We're not even sure if Cain knew what it meant to take someone's life, since murder had never happened before, but we soon learn that he wasn't very fazed by it.

Why did this happen? Jealousy and depression. Cain was both angry and sad at the same time, the Bible says, because G-d had rejected his offering but accepted Abel's. This potent brew of emotions caused Cain to become dangerous.

It wasn't without warning. G-d, seeing that an inner toxic storm was brewing within the first human son ever born, prodded Cain by pointing out, "Sin is crouching at your door; it desires to have you, but you must rule over it" (Genesis 4:7).

Apparently, he couldn't control his emotions. These new, raw feelings were ignited within Cain, who was frustrated that his first outreach to G-d wasn't deemed good enough. So instead of heeding G-d's suggestions to improve his self-awareness, Cain did away with the competition.

Enraged by G-d's preference of Abel's sacrifice over his own, Cain lured his *brother* to a field and killed him—then and there, in cold blood. He thought he had removed the only roadblock between him and G-d. He soon discovered that, quite to the contrary, his act of treachery and his subsequent indifference to his sin would create an insurmountable barrier between him and his Creator.

What is curious about the dramatic story is how G-d responded to this first gruesome murder, somehow animated by apparent religious fervor. Of course, G-d knew exactly what had happened. G-d knows everything. Cain had murdered his brother. G-d could have immediately sent a bolt of lightning from on high to inflict swift justice on the brother who committed the crime; G-d's message to humankind would be unmistakable: murder another human and you're toast. Instead, G-d had a lesson for Cain and a lesson for us, reverberating even to this day.

Rather than confront Cain and demand, "How could you kill your brother?" G-d skipped the divine wrath and instead just asked Cain a simple question: "Where is your brother Abel?" (Genesis 4:9).

By posing the question, G-d did two things.

First, he introduced Cain to his conscience, invoking the voice of truth to preach its own sermon to the heart of the first brother who had murdered his own flesh and blood. Second, G-d also seemed to hint that Cain had some obligation to know Abel's whereabouts. G-d clearly expected Cain to care about his brother. As his big brother he had a responsibility to Abel and to his family—the first nuclear human family in the world.

Cain replied to G-d's question with a question of his own, committing a second sin—no doubt easier because of his first. Cain lied to G-d. "I don't know," he declared and then added defensively, "Am I my brother's keeper?" (Genesis 4:9). For the second time Cain missed the point, another message from G-d, with whom Cain so desperately wanted a close relationship. G-d had already made it clear by the question. Cain was his brother's keeper. That *was* G-d's expectation, which could have served as a lifeline for the sinner.

Finally, G-d indicted Cain for his sin and his apathy, telling him that "your brother's blood cries out to me from the ground" (Genesis 4:10).

Biblical scholars, Jewish and Christian, will continue to link the events surrounding Cain and Abel to core lessons and principles taught throughout scripture, emphasizing every person's obligation to mankind—friend and even foe. This lesson is so important that it's taught within the first five chapters of the Bible. It's reiterated elsewhere, as in Leviticus 19:16, where Moses' words seem to allude to G-d's ancient confrontation with Cain. Hearing still the cry of Abel's blood, Moses teaches, "do not stand idly by the blood of your neighbor."[1]

But Abel was Cain's actual brother. Cain was literally supposed to be his "brother's keeper." How do we know that G-d's question to Cain would also extend beyond our family?

Surely, we might think, *I'm not obligated to care for those whom I don't know, or those with whom I do not have some direct connection, or those whose fate seemingly has no connection to my own fate.*

For our purposes, as religious folks, we might feel obligated to say that we care about the tragedy in Nigeria—or tragedies like it around the world—but do we have some *moral obligation* to actually do something, to get involved? In other words, am I my Nigerian brother's keeper? Even if I don't know him? In our complex world, G-d will certainly understand that it's all I can do to take care of my own, right?

LORD, JUST WHO IS MY BROTHER?

To answer this question, we'll call upon the wisdom of two rabbis from the second century, Rabbi Akiva and Ben Azzai.

The two scholars studied, taught, and lived the Torah amid

the tyranny of the Roman Empire, bereft of the holy temple that had been destroyed a generation earlier. Eventually they would die as martyrs at the hands of the Romans.

One account of Rabbi Akiva's martyrdom finds him standing in front of the Roman judge Tineius Rufus at the very moment the rabbi was required by Jewish law to recite the Shema, the oldest, daily sacred prayer of allegiance to G-d.

The Romans had made the practice illegal, but the rabbi defied the judge to his face and recited it with a smile. "When [Judge] Rufus asked him why he smiled, Akiva replied that all his life he had read the verse, 'and you shall love your G-d with all your heart, all your soul, and all your possessions,' but was never able to fulfill the obligation to love G-d with all his soul—that is, his life—until now."[2]

Rabbi Akiva would bestow for the ages some of Judaism's most quoted texts, which contributed uniquely to Jewish values and practice, both ancient and modern. He is also well known for an oft-quoted and spirited debate that he shared with Ben Azzai about which was the most important principle in the Torah:

"Love your neighbor as yourself" (Leviticus 19:18).
Rabbi Akiva said: "This is the great principle of the Torah."
Ben Azzai said: "This is the record of Adam's line" (Genesis 5:1)—This principle is even greater than that.[3]

One author presents an insight that holds a clue to understanding our moral obligations in our time:

What is Ben Azzai trying to say with his odd quotation from Genesis [*this is the record of Adam's line*]? As is often the case in these texts, it is worthwhile to look at the whole Biblical context of the quoted verses. What Ben Azzai is really after is the way that the verse continued: "This is the record of Adam's line—when G-d created man, He made him in the likeness of G-d; male and female He created them." For Ben Azzai the important point is that *all* human beings are created in G-d's image, and therefore no one person is superior to another; for Akiva the key principle in the Torah is the requirement to love one's fellow human beings. . . . [T]here is something appealing about Akiva's elevation of the emotion of love, and at the same time there is something comforting about Ben Azzai's concept of a just society.[4]

While it may be emphasized more in Judaism than in Christianity, both religions share a foundational principle that influences our theological outlook and helps us define our obligations to our fellow man: we believe, as a Jew and as a Christian, that every single human being is made in the image of G-d himself.

We all come from the same family. As children of Adam, we all share a common humanity, and, therefore, not one of us is better than the other. This is one reason we feel an obligation to look beyond our immediate families, beyond our borders, beyond our common cultures and comfort zones, to keep an eye out and a heart open for our unseen brothers.

This is one reason why the narrative of Cain and Abel, the

amazing assertion of Genesis 1:27 ("In the image of G-d he created them; male and female"), Ben Azzai's powerful insight into Genesis 5:1 ("This is the record of Adam's line"[5]), and the demand of Leviticus 19:16 ("Do not stand idly by the blood of your neighbor"[6]) are so powerfully relevant to our missions.

In this book, we are trying to fulfill a promise we made to ourselves as we sat in stunned silence absorbing the pain and spiritual power of the victims we met in Nigeria. We are driven to be advocates for those who cannot advocate for themselves. The very least we can do for our distant brothers and sisters is to be a voice for the voiceless. And if you've read this far, your conscience—like ours—must now bear responsibility to let them know their cries are silent no more, their tears no longer invisible.

You might feel you need to "rescue those being led away to death; / hold back those staggering toward slaughter" (Proverbs 24:11). But scripture puts on us a moral obligation beyond just expressing this sentiment:

> If you say, "But we knew nothing about this,"
>> does not he who weighs the heart perceive it?
> Does not he who guards your life know it?
>> Will he not repay everyone according to what they have
>> done?" (Proverbs 24:12).

In some sense we are sorry to place on your shoulders the weight of responsibility we have come to bear through our experiences with the suffering people of faith in Nigeria and around the world, but this is precisely what we've aimed to do. This was the promise we made to the victims we sat with.

Now, like us, you can no longer say, "But I did not know." Now you know—as we know—what is happening.

Managing this moral weight is what prompted many ancient scholars to move beyond acknowledging suffering and actually do something to alleviate it. Volumes have been written on the subject through the centuries, but we'll just reboot Leviticus 19:16: "Don't stand idly by the blood of your neighbor."[7] Jewish law—and often Christian tradition—have categorized this command as a *prohibition*, not just an *obligation*. This means the expectation is higher.

It means that abiding by it could, as the rabbis wrote, require significant financial loss, and if an individual has information that might prevent the death of his neighbor, then he is obligated to speak up. One of the great Jewish philosophers of all time, Maimonides (often called Rambam), was both a rabbi and a doctor in Egypt and Morocco in the thirteenth century. His work has been celebrated by intellectuals among many religious communities. Maimonides once said that this command in Leviticus 19:16 even extends to a responsibility "to prevent the loss of someone's property" and not just a person's life.[8]

These are just snippets of volumes of appeals in scripture for followers of G-d to care about others, to always have the suffering of others in our minds.

Elsewhere in Leviticus farmers are instructed to always leave a portion of their field or their vineyard for the poor, or never to collect the grapes that fall to the ground. Then there are the profound demands for justice, such as Isaiah 1:17:

> Learn to do good;
> seek justice,
>> correct oppression;
> bring justice to the fatherless,
>> plead the widow's cause. (ESV)

and Micah 6:8:

> He has told you, O man, what is good;
>> and what does the LORD require of you
> but to do justice, and to love kindness,
>> and to walk humbly with your God? (ESV)

as well as many other inspirational and, frankly, discomfiting calls to action. We think of the words of the prophet Isaiah: "Then I heard the voice of the Lord saying, 'Whom shall I send? And who will go for us?' And I said, 'Here am I. Send me!'" (6:8).

While we approach the question of moral responsibility from two different religious perspectives—as a Jewish rabbi framing his faith from the context of legally proscribed *mitzvot* (actions) and as a Christian pastor seeking to emulate the life of Jesus— somehow we ended up in the same place, responding to the faint echoes of our brothers' pleas.

We draw upon the same Hebrew Bible (what Christians call the Old Testament), whose concepts are often echoed in Christian texts, such as Mark 12:31 ("Love your neighbor as yourself") and Matthew 25:40 ("Whatever you did for one of the least of these brothers and sisters of mine, you did for me"); in the obligations laid out in the letters of the apostle Paul in 1 Corinthians 12:26 ("If one member suffers, all suffer together," ESV) and Galatians 6:10 ("Let us do good to all people, especially to those who belong to the family of believers"); and in James 1:27 ("Religion that is pure and undefiled before G-d the Father is this: to visit orphans and widows in their affliction," ESV) and James 2:26 ("Faith apart from works is dead," ESV).

Jew or Christian, we've been called to make a difference in this world, not only through faith but through deeds. We also received the message from G-d's simple question to Cain about the consequences for apathy and dishonesty with oneself.

And we studied the powerful words of Proverbs 21:13: "Whoever closes his ear to the cry of the poor / will himself call out and not be answered" (ESV). Of course, part of being human is to need the help of others, and scripture warns that a world—or a community, or a family—inhabited by people who don't care for others will be a world of people who will have no one left to care for them.

We remember the words of the Protestant theologian Martin Niemöller, who began as a Nazi sympathizer before becoming a Nazi enemy. He famously said, "First, they came for the socialists, and I did not speak out—because I was not a socialist. Then, they came for the trade unionists, and I did not speak out—because I was not a trade unionist. Then, they came for the Jews, and I did not speak out—because I was not a Jew. Then, they came for me—and there was no one left to speak for me."[9]

THE WORLD YOU WANT TO LIVE IN

Religious or not, this moral imperative presents another challenging question: What kind of world do we want to live in? Our answer may be formed by religious beliefs, but it isn't contingent on them.

Do we want to live in a world where nations as large and influential as Nigeria can maintain the status quo while rendering millions of believers helpless before evildoers? Do we want to live in a world where European diplomats openly negotiate business deals with Iranian mullahs who deny the Nazi Holocaust took place and plot to fulfill Hitler's vision of destroying the Jewish State of Israel? Do we want to live in a world where a country's diplomats sit in the hallowed halls of the United Nations while they allow tyrants in their land to imprison a million Muslims, destroy Christian churches, and make dissidents disappear—as if no one notices or cares?

We are among the fortunate ones to live in the world's freest nation in history—the United States of America—and we have been blessed and empowered with the tools to help shape what type of world we want to live in. As the great Simon Wiesenthal said, "Freedom is not a gift from heaven, it must be earned every day."[10]

Wiesenthal, by the way, knew the cost of the alternative. He had lost eighty-nine members of his family during the Nazi

Holocaust, and when he was liberated from Mauthausen by American soldiers, he weighed less than ninety pounds.[11]

Prior to the horrors of the war and the Nazi genocide, Wiesenthal had completed a degree in architecture, and he certainly could have eventually reaped a small fortune as an architect in postwar Europe. Instead, he invested his life in an entirely different mission. He became the world's foremost Nazi hunter, dedicating every day of his life, surrounded by former Nazis in Vienna, to becoming the unelected ambassador and advocate of six million ghosts—the Jews that the Nazis killed in the Holocaust.

Rabbi Marvin Hier writes that Simon Wiesenthal was

unable to let go of those terrible memories that haunted him. Especially the memory of having chased after the cattle car that carted off his beloved mother to the death camps without her ever knowing of his desperate attempt to run after the train in order to bid her a final farewell.[12]

By the time he died at ninety-six,

this architect from Buchach helped bring hundreds of Nazi war criminals to justice, and not just ordinary criminals. People like Franz Stangle, the commandant of Treblinka; Gustav Wagner, the commandant of Sobibor; and Walter Rauf, the inventor of the mobile gas vans who had murdered hundreds of thousands.[13]

Wiesenthal was once asked, "Why do you do this, and when is it enough?" He replied, "The Nazis almost succeeded at obliterating the concepts of justice, and I must work to revive justice!"

He also expressed these ideas a year before his death in a letter written the day he was awarded the Presidential Medal of Freedom by president Bill Clinton. Wiesenthal penned:

> My cause is justice, not vengeance. My work is for a better tomorrow and a more secure future for our children and grandchildren who will follow us. As a firm believer that each of us are accountable before our creator, I believe that when my life has ended, I shall one day be called to meet up with those who perished and they will undoubtedly ask me, "What have you done?" At that moment, I will have the honor of stepping forward and saying to them, I have never forgotten you.[14]

Simon Wiesenthal knew that creating a just world required dedication, courage, and vigilance, and that we humans are only as strong as our weakest link. How much truer is this today in a hyperglobalized world so entirely interconnected by technology?

As was true with the spread of the invisible coronavirus in 2020, so now it is undeniable that when injustice is allowed to flourish in one place, it will not be long before that injustice touches all of us. Injustice is flourishing in Nigeria and in many other places around the globe. We must do something about it.

If compassion alone doesn't demand your action, then be inspired by your own self-interest to bring to the battle all the unique gifts and skills given to you by G-d. We don't expect anyone, including ourselves, to reorganize our lives to focus exclusively on this crisis and tragedy. We aren't selling all of our worldly possessions and investing everything we have in it. We are just seeking ways to do our share, from where we are, with what we have, to try to make a difference while we can.

That's what we are asking you to do as well. If you do, none of us will be alone to confront the challenges ahead. "It is not your responsibility to finish the work," said the famous Jewish teacher Rabbi Tarfon two thousand years ago, "but you are not free to desist from it."[15]

Nine

WHAT CAN BE DONE TO HELP

*The voice of the drops of blood of your
brother cry out to Me from the ground!*
—GENESIS 4:10[1]

So beyond a *tsk, tsk* or maybe a sermon or two, what exactly
can—or must—we do to degrade the real-time ethnic cleansing gaining momentum toward, G-d forbid, a genocide? What can
be done to ensure that Nigerians won't have to fear their next trip
to their grandmother's house or worry that their homes or places
of worship will be decimated by brutal Boko Haram, the Islamic
State in West Africa, or certain radicalized Fulani militants?

These questions also raise the specter as to whether "democratic" Nigeria can survive its almost daily flaunting of both
the rule of law and the moral foundations of its religions and
civilization.

Writing this book has been an unusual experience for us

because almost daily our in-boxes have been filled with new information, additional lists of victims, and stories that only a heart of stone could withstand. It is what people in the military would call a "live-fire situation."

Today's list came to us from a human rights activist. She sent us a link to an NGO's report titled, "620 Nigerian Christians Hacked to Death in Four Months."[2] Keep in mind that for every Nigerian who is violently killed, thousands more are displaced or kidnapped, and there are many whose homes, businesses, and places of worship are torched. Others' stories are never known and, therefore, never told. This report addresses only one part of Nigeria from January until April 2020. It reads, "The atrocities against Christians have gone unchecked and risen to [an] alarming [degree] with the country's security forces and concerned political actors looking the other way or colluding with the Jihadists. Houses burnt or destroyed during the period are in their hundreds; likewise, dozens of Christian worship and learning centers."[3]

To use another analogy that we have used before, the house is on fire, and it is a "five-alarm-fire."[4] These atrocities occur at the hands of not only infamous and well-known terrorists such as Boko Haram but also increasingly Fulani militants—not to be confused with the millions of peaceful Fulani—whose acts of terror continue with impunity because of unmistakable, undeniable, unjustifiable government indifference. In fact, we received a communiqué from a senior Nigerian official who wanted to alert us that the government had been aggressively going after Boko Haram (probably because of intense international pressure).

A recent military campaign—during Ramadan—has had at least some effect, prompting Boko Haram's leader, Shekau, to produce a dramatic video in which he prays for G-d's help. His pleas are accompanied by weeping, "May Allah protect us from [the Nigerian Army's] evil." He continues, "We forsook our parents, uncles and aunties to practice Your true religion. It is because of your religion that we placed knife on . . . necks. . . . Oh Allah give us victory."[5]

Maybe such sustained military interventions will degrade the threat from Boko Haram, though we must confess that past, hollow precedents have made us suspicious. We question whether the Nigerian government has the will to complete the task or whether this is just an effort to temporarily pacify critics and incentivize the terrorists and their supporters to back off—for a while.

But even if Nigerian forces somehow suddenly succeed in finishing off Boko Haram, what then? Is there any game plan to defeat ISIS in West Africa or the Fulani militants? In that same text message from the senior government official, he said this about the Fulani: "The good news is that the Fulani attacks have also diminished because of the coronavirus."

Really? Social distancing is going to save the nation? This is wishful thinking as a blueprint to defeat the Fulani extremists. No, protecting millions of law-abiding Nigerians from the ongoing attacks of these thugs will demand a real action plan, national consensus, and political will from the elite.

It's all déjà vu to us.

Once again the leadership of a country (and global allies

of Nigeria) are all too comfortable inhabiting a territory called *Denial*. If plans exist to forestall the next chapters of the Fulani thugs, it will be a shock to them and to us.

WHAT THE INTERNATIONAL COMMUNITY CAN DO

What narrative will be memorialized in tomorrow's headlines? Writers Akpor-Robaro and Lanre-Babalola supply a preview in the *IOSR Journal of Humanities and Social Science*: "The scale of deaths attributable to Fulani herdsmen attacks across the country far outweigh the amount of deaths that had been caused by any terrorist group or militant group that currently exist or ever existed in Nigeria, including the notorious Boko Haram insurgents."[6]

So we must now address the core issue: Can anything stop the next jihad? And, if so, what role can we play?

The United States, the United Kingdom, the European Union, and other countries must immediately review all aid and assistance to the country. Nigeria annually receives billions of dollars in aid from various countries around the world. While much of that aid is directed toward lifesaving humanitarian assistance, some of it is specifically designed to support Nigeria's security needs, its democracy, and its infrastructure. Of course governments should not cease providing humanitarian assistance, but all other money flowing into Nigeria ought to be put under an immediate and expedited review to ensure that Western largesse is addressing and achieving its intended purpose—otherwise known as *transparency*. While no one is naive enough to believe Nigeria's deeply embedded corruption will suddenly and magically disappear, such a financial move would serve as a shot across the bow of this cancerous situation, which has been the unacceptable status quo for too long. Perhaps the US and the UK could lead the way in linking funds to verifiable results on the ground. Other contributing donor nations could be invited to join with each government, assigning a special envoy to coordinate and oversee these activities in real time.

The continuing international debate over the reasons for the violence must be replaced by a firm demand that the Nigerian government act to stop all organized attacks against Christians and other innocents. The issues facing Nigeria are complex and multifaceted. But whether the attacks are primarily criminal or terrorist in nature, it's time for the world to be clear that significant religious and ideological components are in play. Denying this brutal reality is an insult to the memory of the victims killed because of their faith and makes it impossible to create effective strategies against the burgeoning violence. On behalf of the survivors and the endangered communities, we must demand that debates over causation cannot be used as excuses for inaction. The collective voice of nations and experts must move beyond intellectual and diplomatic reflections to demand that the Nigerian government take immediate and sustained action to finally protect its own citizens and to hold perpetrators legally culpable for their atrocities.

The international community needs to put—and keep—this issue on the forefront of the human rights agenda so that every atrocity—and every government failure to end the violent attacks—is denounced. We were astonished to see how rarely embassies in Abuja, international leaders, and other governments actually speak out against atrocities committed in Nigeria. It is essential that the powerful light of global exposure be shone upon the murderers and their victims for all to see. And the voices of outrage bearing accurate information about these human rights abuses taking place in Africa's largest democracy need to be clear, consistent, and forceful. Those leaders responsible, directly or indirectly, should be sanctioned relentlessly.

The international community must help the silent, anonymous victims find their voices and be empowered to share their narratives at the UN, on Capitol Hill, through social media, and on every major news media network. This book is a small effort to put a human face on mind-numbing statistics. We have tried to give a voice to some, but thousands of others suffer in silence. Only when NGOs, international organizations, governments, and private individuals provide opportunities for victims to be heard is there any chance of ensuring that Nigeria's institutions—from the executive branch to the military to the justice system—will awaken to their responsibilities. There is a time for reflection and debate, and there is a time for deeds and actions. How many more will have to pay the ultimate price for corruption, indifference, and hypocrisy?

The international community must help address the inconsistencies in Nigeria's democracy and the inadequacies in its

government, including in its constitution. Nigeria could not have a democratic election without the robust assistance of the international community. Such assistance must continue, but it must be optimized to address the inconsistencies in the political system, including the interaction between the federal and state governments as well as the constitution's privileging of Islamic communities. Of course religious freedom for all must include equal protection under federal law for *all* religious communities. Nigeria must remain a secular democracy with religious freedom enshrined in law and practice. Islamization—or even Christianization—of the country must be rejected. A lack of inclusive governance in Nigeria is an existential threat to its democracy. The country must work to include true representation from every region and ethnic group with equal treatment and equal justice for all, whatever their religious affiliation or lack thereof.

The international community must demand that Nigeria address unhelpful interference in its affairs by outside malign actors. While this subject hasn't been our principal focus, it is important to recognize that various malign actors have been active, and are active, in Nigeria. These include Iranian efforts to foment a Nigerian Hezbollah, led by Sheikh Ibrahim Yaqoub El Zakzaky; the direct and indirect, as well as past and present, funding of extremists by groups affiliated with Turkey and certain Gulf nations; and the expansive financial investment of the People's Republic of China in Nigeria's industry and infrastructure, which is often leveraged to provide political cover against the West's efforts to promote human rights, democracy, and the rule of law.

WHAT NIGERIANS CAN DO

Set up an independent inquiry. The Nigerian government must set up a mechanism to provide fully independent analysis of the atrocities committed, help determine the responsible parties, and offer clear and binding recommendations to address the inadequacies.

Provide robust security to protect vulnerable communities and crush insurgents. It is clear that when Nigeria has decided to address insurgents, they have been capable of reducing the threat and the needless tragedies and suffering. When President Trump met with President Buhari in 2018, Trump publicly confronted him at the White House for the atrocities committed against vulnerable communities in his country. The Nigerian government suddenly embarked upon a mission to contain terrorists. That surge of activity helped curtail the terrorists' advance, just as a similar surge had helped during the presidency of Goodluck Jonathan when he hired private military contractors to pursue Boko Haram. Nigeria's military needs to be trained to act against both Boko Haram as well as militant Fulani tribesmen. But the government has too often chosen not to act.

Prosecute to the fullest extent of the law every perpetrator and every leader whose hate speech enables these crimes. Especially as it relates to the attacks by Fulani tribesmen, almost no one is ever prosecuted in Nigeria for these crimes. While Boko Haram (and other) terrorists are sometimes caught and prosecuted, they are often released in exchange for kidnapped civilians. The Nigerian government must start prosecuting criminals, whatever the cost, and they should appeal to the international community for help to withstand—not appease—terrorists' blackmail.

Provide financial assistance to communities needing to be rebuilt. Nigeria's oil wealth ought to be utilized to rebuild communities that have been destroyed. Rebuilding impacted Christian communities is one of the best ways to send a signal to the terrorists and thugs that Nigeria rejects ethnic cleansing.

Address inadequacies in the constitution and laws. As stated above, Nigeria's laws and constitution must be reformed, and a coalition of Christian and Islamic politicians ought to be formed to achieve this aim. We appreciate that the government has invested energy and resources in creating various plans to address the existing competition for resources, but it is time for those plans to be fully implemented. A version of this might look like the National Livestock Transformation Plan created by the National Economic Council. Until now, there has been too much talk and too little action.

Hold state governments accountable when their policies violate fundamental freedoms. It's time for federal and state governments to cease scapegoating one another to deflect responsibility as the tragedies pile up. Nigeria's federal system must be fully implemented to ensure that the national and state governments are fulfilling their constitutional duties in a spirit of mutual cooperation and social harmony.

Promote substantive multifaith engagement. The Nigerian government must find a way to substantively involve the country's religious communities in working toward a shared vision and a way forward. They should be seen working together on local and national levels and among every stratum of society. We found that too often leaders of religious communities were only talking *at* one another and rarely talking *with* one another. Religion can be a tool for division, but it can also be a powerful balm for national healing. Religious leaders in Nigeria may be even more important than their political counterparts in forging hope for a better future. The government can create the modalities for such activities, and the media can help educate young Nigerians that they can embrace their national identity while proudly carrying on their religious traditions.

Immediately address the growing scandal and emergency of children out of school and on the streets. When we learned that over a million Nigerian children are on the streets, we knew that these children could be the easiest recruiting targets for extremist and terrorist groups. A country is especially obligated to care for its vulnerable children, and Nigeria must immediately make it its number one priority getting children— the nation's most precious resource—off the streets and back in schools.

End corruption and stop facilitating extortion. The country must stop acceding to the demands of terrorists and criminals whose extortion schemes have cost tens of millions of dollars, and whose successful results have spawned a market for kidnapping that is unparalleled in other parts of the world. Nigeria must cease paying ransoms, and it must once and for all end corruption on all levels, beginning within the halls of political power.

WHAT YOU CAN DO

Internalize the stories of the victims and tell those stories to others. Read the stories in this book and those published in the media many times. Internalize the feelings and experiences of the victims, and then tell those stories to others. Tell them to your clergy, in your communities of worship, to your family and friends. Post on social media about them, and make sure that your circle of influence is aware. Be a voice for the voiceless.

Give to organizations helping those in need. Many great organizations are advocating for human rights and providing for the needs of those who have been affected around the world. Give something, even if it's small, to help.

Pray for the victims. Pray regularly and often for the victims, for those in harm's way, and for those who have the power to address the growing problem. When you do, pray like you hope someone would pray for you—as though it were *your* family or church, *your* town or community, or *your* loved ones whose lives were threatened and livelihood taken or denied. As people of faith, we believe that there is power when one appeals to G-d on behalf of the vulnerable.

Demand action from elected officials and human rights and religious NGOs. Make sure your elected officials hear from you regularly and often. Email them, call them, show up in their local and national offices. Elected leaders respond to the demand of constituents, and in our advocacy we have seen again and again how effective it is when our politicians feel the direct demands of the people. Be sure your information is accurate, and make it clear that you expect them to be part of the solution and not prolong the disastrous status quo.

Consider sponsoring visits by victims and survivors of terror in Nigeria and by clergy—Christian and Muslim—who have the courage to stand up for their neighbors. Never underestimate the potential impact of authentic voices of the faithful. If nothing else is achieved, they will bring back the message that they are not forgotten!

"NEVER AGAIN" IS NOW

At the height of the 2014 atrocities by ISIS in Iraq and Syria, Hollywood celebrities Mark Burnett and Roma Downey decided they had to do something about it. They sent a personal note to their friend Cardinal Donald Wuerl, the archbishop of Washington, DC, at the time, as they eventually did to many religious leaders around the world. They lamented their fears for the fate of the Christians, Yazidis, and others (including many Muslims) who were being massacred in Iraq and Syria. Burnett and Downey decided to *act* in addition to simply *praying*, and their letter left an impression on the cardinal in their nation's capital, which is perhaps the most powerful city on earth.

Their voice echoed loudly a few days later when, after conducting the opening convocation for the Catholic University of America, the stately cardinal left his script and made a sudden emotional appeal to the thousands viewing in person and online. Pained by the injustice of the persecution of the faithful, he told the students, professors, and parents that something had to be done about the women and children being sold as slaves, the beheadings, and the desecration of sacred sites. Burnett and Downey's appeal to their friend ignited the cardinal's plea to thousands:

> We simply cannot in conscience ignore [this].
>
> Often we're asked, How is it possible that in human history atrocities occur? They occur for two reasons: Because there are those prepared to commit them and there are those who remain silent. . . .
>
> Where are these voices? . . . Why a silence?
>
> I think each one of us has at least the power to raise our voice and be in solidarity with people distant from us, unknown to us.[7]

Those are the final words in *Defying ISIS*, released during the height of ISIS' power in Iraq and Syria. Those aren't words that one hopes would ever have to be repeated to appeal to mankind's conscience, but evil is challenging all of us again, this time in a different part of the world.

The truth is that the atrocities in Nigeria, and the broader region, were also raging when ISIS established its short-lived but disastrous caliphate. But the terror in Africa happened almost entirely in the shadows, unbeknownst to a largely indifferent world.

So we finish this book as *Defying ISIS* concluded in 2015, with those same words from the former archbishop of Washington, DC: "Why a silence?"

But we shall also add more words—not from a famous and powerful religious leader but from a decent person overwhelmed by the daily brutalities staining her homeland. She also uttered her words in Washington, DC, to an audience at the National Press Club in 2019:

> Nearly every single day I wake up with text messages [from] Nigeria, such as this morning, "Herdsmen stab 49-year-old farmer in Ogan." . . . Frankly, I don't know where Ogan is. I don't know this 49-year-old farmer. But when I wake up and read that, I weep. It's the conscience of all of us around the world that needs to weep when we read that. If you get that every single day and that's how you wake up, you realize that it is up to us to do something.[8]

What would G-d say? He already had his say, right there at the beginning of Genesis:

> Then G-d said unto Cain, "Where is your brother, Abel?"
> And Cain said, "I don't know! Am I my brother's keeper?"
> And G-d said: "What have you done? The voice of the drops of blood of your brother cry out to Me from the ground!"
> (4:9–10, authors' paraphrase of the Hebrew text)

Now, we cannot blame G-d. We can only pray for his intervention and mercy, and we know that he will do his share if we, as his junior partners here on earth, do ours.

So we appeal to you—believers and those who do not yet

believe: do what we all know is right. We can and we must, individually and collectively, stand up for the suffering of our brothers and sisters.

Now.

Epilogue

A CONVERSATION ON HELPING SAVE LIVES FOR FIFTY YEARS

*O*n the day we completed the manuscript of this book, the two of us hopped on Zoom for a little over an hour, and I (Johnnie Moore) interviewed Rabbi Abraham Cooper as he reflected on his fifty years of speaking out against injustice. We had a powerful conversation, which is summarized here.

JOHNNIE MOORE: Rabbi Abe, maybe we can talk a bit about what led us to Nigeria, but you've been a voice for justice for your entire life, all over the world. What led you to invest your life in speaking to those in power and for those who are persecuted or oppressed?

RABBI COOPER: Remember, I was born five years after the end of World War II. My father was a saintly person. He was a teacher, a Hebrew teacher. We were lovers of this fledgling state called Israel. Always a lot of singing on the Sabbath; my father had a great voice. Our apartment was modest—one bedroom.

I was basically a clueless kid, but my parents gave me a

great gift by sending me to one of the elite Jewish schools called Yeshivah of Flatbush, in Brooklyn. It was an amazingly rich Jewish environment, Zionist environment, but also an American environment. I was a Brooklyn Dodgers fan. I remember the trolleys and all of it. Sports became an obsession, and baseball was the centerpiece of my life.

JOHNNIE MOORE: How aware were you of the Holocaust as a kid?

RABBI COOPER: One day I met a new cousin whose family didn't speak much English. His parents were clearly from Europe, and they were actually the first Holocaust survivors I had ever met. Other than that, there was no immediacy about the Holocaust. But later on, some of my teachers were survivors. Stop and think about it—they may have been fifteen years out from what they had experienced. The absolute horror. Many of these people didn't sleep at night because of the memories. Then there was the Eichmann trial that aired on ABC TV. I think I was eleven.

JOHNNIE MOORE: You still remember seeing the Eichmann trial?

RABBI COOPER: Well, not all of the details, but I remember the clips that were shown of the mass graves that were uncovered, of the skeletal people. Holocaust Memorial Day back then was usually April 20, which is the anniversary of the beginning of the 1943 Warsaw Ghetto Uprising. There was no academic research yet. There was just raw pain. Most of which was not thrust in my young face, but you could sense something powerful and dark was lurking—it was there. In a rich Jewish environment, as you got older, your teachers began to teach you more, and you'd have some more context.

Memory is at the heart of Jewish life.

I remember my friend, a cantor, who grew up in a suburb of Tel Aviv, and he would tell me that on the hot summer nights—in the 1950s and '60s before there was air-conditioning—people would leave their windows open and you could hear the screams throughout the neighborhood almost every night of Holocaust survivors reliving what they went through.

JOHNNIE MOORE: Wow.

RABBI COOPER: Then along came a very controversial guy named Rabbi Meir Kahane in New York. He created the Jewish Defense League, and he was the person who coined the term "never again."

A righteous anger fueled Kahane that did not cool till the day he died. His loud and rash activism catapulted him to a key leadership role in the early years of the struggle to save Soviet Jewry. That anger touched our generation.

So as I came of age, I learned that there were three million Jews trapped in the Soviet Union. It was the height of the Cold War. Forget about Gorbachev or détente—this was when Americans were building bomb shelters in their backyards, when everyone assumed that there could very well be a nuclear confrontation with these bad, powerful guys.

JOHNNIE MOORE: While it wasn't that long ago, a lot of people in my generation (Jew or Christian) honestly aren't educated enough on that era. Can you tell me more about the Jews that were stuck in the Soviet Union?

RABBI COOPER: Some of them were Holocaust survivors. They were trapped because the system identified a Jew not only by a nationality in the Soviet Union, but also by a religion. That meant that their internal passport had the word *Jew* stamped on it. The Soviet Union was officially an atheistic state. No Jewish schools were allowed to function; no one could have contact with their loved ones in the West. After Israel's smashing victory in the 1967 Six-Day War, a sense of Jewish pride and self-awareness burst forth, but the Soviet Union didn't allow anyone to migrate anywhere, let alone to Israel—after all, who would ever want to leave the Workers' Socialist paradise?

So three million Jews were effectively trapped. You couldn't leave being a Jew, and—because there was no freedom of religion—you couldn't live as a Jew. Even in the post-Stalinist era, everyone was justifiably paranoid. They were afraid to do anything that would bring official attention or detention to themselves, or they might even be sent off to the gulag. In the twenty-first century, with the implosion of the Communist Iron Curtain, it is hard to fathom the degree of fear that the Soviet system instilled in everyone.

Some of us were screaming at our parents' generation, "You didn't do enough. Whatever it is that you did wasn't enough during the Holocaust. We lost six million. How can the Jewish people possibly survive if three million more Jews perish from a cultural genocide in the Soviet Union?"

Some people would look at us and say, "Look, you can't take on the Soviet Union. Let our leaders try quiet diplomacy." But quiet diplomacy didn't save the six million during World War II.

JOHNNIE MOORE: But somehow your generation took on the Soviet Union anyhow?

RABBI COOPER: Here's where the American part comes in.

Remember what was cooking in American society then: you had the civil rights movement, Vietnam and Cambodia, and all of that stuff, and a black pastor named Martin Luther King Jr. steps forward with an American version—an American *religious* version—of Gandhi and says, "Oh no, I'm an American, and despite the evils that threaten us, I believe in the goodness of people." He quotes Isaiah and says, "We can do better. We are better. We have to figure out a way to change the status quo. This cannot remain. We will overcome."

Dr. King was a friend of the Jews and a supporter of Israel. He always used Zionist language, and one of the powerful animating forces of his movement was a call to "make it to the promised land." His message resonated deeply with Jewish survivors, and some of the rabbis who walked with him had actually escaped the Nazis. Younger Jews, like me, who were inspired by MLK, were saying, "Hey, wait a second. There may be a way to try to do something that's never been done before. Maybe there is a possibility. Even if not, we must try."

JOHNNIE MOORE: What did you do?

RABBI COOPER: I was inspired as a teenager by a slightly older young man, Glenn Richter, who cofounded the Student Struggle for Soviet Jewry. He wasn't waiting for the approval of the formal leadership of the Jewish community. It wasn't a revolt against our elders; it was a simple message—"We're not waiting for you."

If there were only thirty people who showed up to the pre-Passover Soviet Jewry seder in front of the Soviet Mission to the United Nations in New York—so be it. Twenty-five or thirty years later, however, 250,000 people showed up in Washington, DC, for a Freedom Sunday for Soviet Jews. But it started small with a few people. We were galvanized by the Holocaust, inspired by the Jewish State of Israel, connected to the anger of a Meir Kahane, and encouraged by the moral power of Dr. Martin Luther King Jr. As Jews we were taught to believe in miracles; as Americans we believed that anything was possible—so we had to try.

For me, it was a number of strands: a deep and profound love of Israel and humanity, anger at the genocide inflicted by the Nazis on my people, and inspiration from watching the biblical-style heroism of Dr. Martin Luther King Jr. All of it.

Three million Jews were trapped behind the Iron Curtain. We didn't know yet how we could help them, but we were going to help them. The State of Israel had worked diligently since its founding to compile a list of every Jew in the Soviet Union—a true "mission impossible" in the secretive years of Stalin and his successors. The point was that every single Jewish life mattered. So we students tried to do our share—demonstrating, holding vigils, working to educate our peers, and trying to motivate our elders to urge our governments to put Soviet Jewry on the world's agenda.

JOHNNIE MOORE: But you eventually went to the Soviet Union yourself, right? That was a pretty courageous thing to do.

RABBI COOPER: Well, I just reached the point one day where I went to one of my mentors and said, "If I have to go to one more demonstration and protest in front of the UN, I'm going to go out of my mind."

I think I was twenty-one when I decided I had to go to the Soviet Union and see it for myself. If it was really that bad, then I would come back and do more; and if it wasn't, I had enough already.

So that led to the life-changing experience in September and October 1972.

JOHNNIE MOORE: Give us some context for that time.

RABBI COOPER: Historically it was just before the reelection of Nixon to his fateful second term. I went with a lifelong friend from Brooklyn, David Koenigsberg. We went to the Soviet Union for four weeks, and we gave everything we had to the Refuseniks, coming home with no money and only the clothes we were wearing.

One of the unexpected takeaways was that I forever became a patriot of the United States of America. I got on that Pan American plane to come home, and when I was leaving I saw the US flag and told the stewardess, "I just want to kiss the flag."

So my education about the uniqueness and majesty of America was four weeks in the Soviet Union!

JOHNNIE MOORE: It must have been astonishing to experience the difference between the United States and the Soviet Union at the height of the Cold War.

RABBI COOPER: Everything about growing up in America is, "Oh, if you don't like something . . . stand up and change it." You don't like the food? Open your own restaurant.

In the Soviet Union, when you sat down in a state-run restaurant, there was one menu—and nothing on the printed menu was ever available. You ate what you were served, and you never ever complained. Back in the bad old days, *anyone* with the chutzpah to stand up and be an individual was going to be in trouble.

Even though Stalin was already gone, Soviets still were Soviets—and everybody was afraid. Older people who had managed to survive Stalin weren't taking any chances. They had loved ones who had disappeared into the gulag. Maybe they were still in Siberia?

In some ways the government didn't have to push that hard because people were basically beaten into submission. More than twenty million were dead from defeating the Nazis. Then you had another twenty million who disappeared into the gulag. The numbers were staggering. The twentieth century was one of the bloodiest in human history, maybe the bloodiest.

Just experiencing that system—and seeing the shabbiness of the world's other superpower—was unbelievable. We were there not long after the death and destruction wreaked on these people by two of the worst murderous dictators in history—Stalin and Hitler. You could talk to people everywhere who had lived through it. Virtually every adult was a survivor of those unspeakably brutal and tragic years.

As for our experiences, the KGB succeeded in scaring us to death.

When you came to a hotel, they'd say, "Can I please have your passport and ticket?" You were never sure if you were going to get them back. You were in "good hands with *all state!*" The KGB was everywhere, listening to everything, following you everywhere. Heck, even the blonde tour guide was KGB.

JOHNNIE MOORE: What did you learn there?

RABBI COOPER: So this is where I discovered an important truth. I experienced it in a profound way, and that truth is why I knew we had to go to Nigeria.

When I traveled to the Soviet Union, I thought I was dedicated to that cause and movement, and we prayed for them, and we went to lobby on Capitol Hill, and maybe we even got arrested (yes, I was once arrested in DC, and I didn't like it very much). And we had gone to the Soviet Union to help "save" these people.

Turns out that those people we were exposed to— whether they were scientists or custodians—were unflinching, modest *heroes*. They were ready to pay any price just to be able to say, "I'm a free person. I can make choices in life. I don't want to live here anymore. I want to go home to my homeland of Israel."

We thought we came to help them, and obviously we brought certain things to them, and we took out certain information, but what an education and what a humbling and inspiring experience it was for us. It has stayed with me ever since.

We came to help them, but they helped and transformed us.

I remember in the Sabbath before Yom Kippur meeting an elderly Jew who told me that he had survived the two worst tyrants in history—Gitler (he couldn't pronounce the *H* in Russian) and Stalin—but now with a strong Israel, he wasn't afraid anymore.

Day after day, city after city, we were astonished by each of the Jews we met. We were exposed to a level of spiritual and personal heroism you can't get from a book or a headline or someone else's speech.

So we convinced ourselves that we needed to go there and sit with these people but that we also had a moral obligation to become a platform for their silenced cries for freedom. This meant that, in the era before the internet, you went around to speak or do whatever you could do to encourage your peers to *do something* to help too.

That experience never left me.

JOHNNIE MOORE: So why Nigeria?

RABBI COOPER: When I heard these stories, horrible stories (and we just got another ten in today's email), my first reaction was, "Horrible!" But you reach a certain point when you say to yourself, "These innocent people's silent cries aren't being heard. Isn't there *something* I can do?"

It reminds me of another inspiration, Simon Wiesenthal, of blessed memory.

When we talk about Simon, we have to remember that he experienced the ultimate—things we can't even understand and a degree of loss that's incomprehensible. Somehow he emerged from hell and decided in the months and years after World War II that "Jews being murdered in Europe was nothing new. But the scope of what just happened—what we just experienced—was something completely different, and we as Jews have an obligation to see that it never happens again to our people or to anyone else."

I myself watched, when in Simon's presence in Vienna or Oslo, all sorts of voiceless victims and minority groups struggling to have their pain and narrative acknowledged were drawn to Simon like a magnet. They understood that this man, a survivor who moved way beyond victimhood, had a message and a sense of solidarity that would help them move forward.

Mr. Wiesenthal was a mentor to many of us, and it has been the great honor of my life to work alongside the founder of the Wiesenthal Center, Rabbi Marvin Hier, to help carry on his legacy.

When you do this work, you don't give up who you are or your loyalties to your own people. You don't have to say that every human rights violation is Auschwitz. In fact, you have an obligation to safeguard the uniqueness of the Shoah [the Holocaust].

But at the end of the day, if you mourn what happened at Auschwitz and you're bitter that so many innocent people could have been saved, then you have a responsibility to respond to new injustices that beset our world. As Mr. Wiesenthal would frequently say, "Jews were often the first victims of injustice; they have never been the last."

So when you hear that they are using gas chambers to improve the poison gas that the North Korean regime is selling to Syria and Iraq and others, you get yourself to Korea and figure out what in the world is going on. When you learn that Saddam used poison gas to murder five thousand Kurds, you find a way to pray over their mass grave. When you hear about what's happened in Sudan or in the Middle East in recent years, or what's happening in Nigeria today, you go. You get involved. You try to do something. Sometimes just showing up and listening to the voiceless is reason enough to make the journey.

Why?

In my case, partly because I carry on Simon Wiesenthal's name, but mainly because G-d calls us to be a voice for the voiceless, to help the oppressed and the vulnerable. We Jews believe that the divine spark—the image of G-d himself—is in every human being.

JOHNNIE MOORE: Everywhere I've gone with you, even in Nigeria, I've found a small, thriving Jewish presence, and they all seem to be in this fight for justice despite the diversity of global Jewry. I wish every Christian could see what I've seen in the Jewish communities of the world.

RABBI COOPER: One of the great secrets of Jewish identity and Jewish survival is that the synagogue is like the local spiritual Jewish embassy, and the prayer book is your passport.

I was once in Paris on the anniversary of my father's passing, and what do you do on the anniversary? You have to lead the prayers in the evening, morning, and afternoon. I told my colleague Shimon Samuels, "You got to find me a minyan [prayer meeting] early enough," because I think we had to go see the French president or minister of justice later that day.

He says, "Well, the good news is, just behind the hotel I put you in, there is a minyan." And sure enough, in the next little building in the back was a little, modest synagogue. I walked in, and there were nine Algerian Jews.

None of these people worked in the fashion industry, okay? These guys were rough-and-tumble—and nobody spoke English.

Culturally, I had absolutely no connection to these people. They loved football; I was a baseball fan. They spoke French and Arabic; I'm a New Yorker. Do the math. But I was the tenth person to arrive, and in Judaism you have to have ten people to have a minyan for a group to pray. And as it turned out, there were four other people in the year of their mourning.

So everybody brightens up because you can't say Kaddish [mourners' prayer] for your loved one without a quorum. My presence as the tenth man meant we could honor all of our loved ones.

At that moment we became a community, and for the next forty-two minutes, even though there were some slight variances in the prayer service and certainly in the accents, it didn't make a difference. We were just one family. We said our mourners' prayers at the end. The minute it was over and you took off your tefillin and the prayer shawl, it was nine Algerians and an American in Paris . . . but we were all Jews.

Even in the Soviet Union, as you know, because you've now been there with me a few times, I have a soft spot for Azerbaijan, and especially Baku, where I spent part of the Sukkot festival during my visit in 1972.

Despite bordering Iran, Turkey, and Russia, and being under constant attacks from Armenia, Azerbaijan is a safe country with a vibrant religious life and a thriving Jewish community. Like Iran, it's a Shia-majority country, yet it has diplomatic relations with Israel. Sunni and Shia Muslims pray together there. Evangelical and orthodox Christians work together. And Jews, in a 96 percent Muslim country, have no fear of walking in the streets with a *kippah* on their heads (unlike Germany or France these days). This shows what can change because, when I first visited, it was part of the Soviet Union. Even then, Jews persevered there.

We had an unbelievable experience in 1972 with a blind, elderly rabbi, a giant in Talmud. Though blind, he knew the entire thing—everything in the Jewish lexicon. Everything by heart. This man would have been a topflight professor or head of yeshiva anywhere else in the world. But he was in the Soviet Union.

Then there were Jews who worshiped in total secrecy or gathered "unofficially," as some Christians do today in parts of the Middle East and China. So we were in Baku's only official synagogue, and someone there told us, "By the way, there is another synagogue in the area."

I said, "Really?"

"Yeah. It's unofficial," they said. "The Mountain Jews pray there."

"Who?" I asked.

They replied, "Yeah, the Mountain Jews. You don't know the Mount Jews? There's a community of Jews here, and they've been here for centuries, isolated up in the mountains."

Without hesitation, David and I left to seek them out.

It wasn't so easy, and I'm not sure we lost our KGB handlers, but we managed to get there. We arrived as two boys from Brooklyn, and the people there looked sort of semi-Asian—Turkish, really, Turkic. People wearing clothes that have fit them for decades maybe.

And their leader was speaking from the center platform, which we call the bema. He was preaching at these people at the top of his lungs in a language we had never heard. It wasn't Russian. We didn't know what he was saying. We didn't know what language he was speaking. It turned out it was a Turkic dialect, something that's unique to them. He was almost screaming!

We quietly found two seats in the front, and we were just sitting there. It was our act of solidarity. We had no way whatsoever to connect to these Jews. But after the sermon, they went back to the prayer service, they opened the ark [where they store the Torah], and they took out the Five Books of Moses.

It so happens my friend David is a Kohain. He's a direct descendant of the first Jewish priest, Aaron, which means he got to read the first blessing—he will be "called to the

Torah." So they opened the biblical parchment, and there it was—the same weekly portion of Scripture that all Jews read in Shabbat around the world. Despite their isolation in the Soviet Union, they were in exactly the same spot in Scripture as every single synagogue in Israel, Toronto, Melbourne, Singapore, Mumbai. Who knew?

Now when I meet young Jews in the former Soviet Union—in the free country of Azerbaijan—and I tell them stories about their communities and their city of fifty years ago, they look at me as though I'm out of my mind or talking about another country or another solar system. And, in a sense, they're right because that whole generation is nearly gone.

It reminds us just how important memory is—to know what it is you have and what can be lost. Azerbaijan also shows that nations, not just individuals, can change. Today any Jew can take a flight from the former Soviet capital of Baku directly to Tel Aviv. It's unbelievable, but it took brave local Jews standing up for their G-d-given rights, and it took a generation of activists willing to shine a light on injustice . . . and in the case of Azerbaijan, it took a leader (the current president, whom we know well) willing to do what needed to be done to free his people from tyranny and fix inequities.

Yes, I learned how to become an American patriot when I saw what the alternative was. When I experienced it, when I saw it not only through the eyes of Jews but through the glazed-over eyes of the general population of the Soviet Union, I understood the difference between socialism in theory and socialism in practice.

Gorbachev would be the first Soviet leader who would understand that no government—however powerful—could forever own the souls of its people.

JOHNNIE MOORE: And of Nigeria?

RABBI COOPER: Well, it wasn't just the stories of the atrocities. It was the light I saw in faces—the strength of the suffering people that we met . . . the light of faith and of hope. What a humbling experience. What an overpowering experience.

And it takes a lot to ignite my Jewish guilt. You know, I'm an American Jew who was born in Brooklyn. I'm not very big on guilt.

Well, sometimes you are exposed to spiritual giants. It could be someone who didn't know a Hebrew *A* from a *B*, as they said of the great Rabbi Akiva (whom we wrote about), who became one of Judaism's great sages. Or it could be a woman in Nigeria who is still in mourning for her world that's been destroyed around her, and she probably only has one dress—but when she speaks of her faith, she speaks as a giant.

JOHNNIE MOORE: Any final word?

RABBI COOPER: Understand one thing: I don't know if we are going to succeed in helping these people, but I know we will be much better people for trying. I just hope that other people will take the same journey to care.

ACKNOWLEDGMENTS

*T*his book would not have been possible without the help of many people but especially Emmanuel Ogebe of the US Nigeria Law Group, whose tireless efforts have inspired us and whose practical help made it possible for us to sit with those who have suffered the most.

We also would like to thank Dr. Richard Ikiebe, Stephen Enada, Kyle Abts, and their team at the International Committee on Nigeria, whose research and guidance played an absolutely indispensable role in our work.

We thank US Secretary of State Mike Pompeo and the White House's National Security Council for having such interest in our advocacy.

We thank key senior leaders in the Nigerian government who have spoken to us sincerely about the challenges that their nation faces.

We thank Rabbi Marvin Hier, dean and founder of the Simon Wiesenthal Center, whose vision of a more just world helped inspire and enable this journey.

We also thank the Simon Wiesenthal Center's own Rabbi Yitzchok Adlerstein for his work building bridges between Jews and other religious communities, which also introduced us to each other several years ago. We are also grateful for Rabbi Adlerstein's brilliant theological and philosophical insights, which have helped shape our advocacy in many ways.

We thank the victims who were willing to trust us with their stories.

And, of course, we thank our families for their support and sacrifice as we have wandered the world trying to make something good out of it for future generations.

A special thanks to all those who read the manuscript early and provided helpful notes, and also for the editing assistance provided by Virginia Peay and Shelby Cook.

NOTES

Prologue

1. Rabbi Lord Jonathan Sacks, "How to End the Wars of Hatred," Rabbi Sacks (website), June 12, 2015, https://rabbisacks.org /how-to-end-the-wars-of-hatred/.
2. Mishnah Avot 1.2.

Introduction

1. Winston Churchill, "The War Situation: House of Many Mansions," International Churchill Society, accessed July 1, 2020, https://winstonchurchill.org/resources/speeches/1940 -the-finest-hour/the-war-situation-house-of-many-mansions/.

Chapter 1: The Perpetrators

1. Reuters, "Suspected Boko Haram Fighters Kill at Least 30 in Nigeria," *New York Times*, February 10, 2020, https://www .nytimes.com/2020/02/10/world/africa/nigeria-boko-haram .html.
2. Bukola Adebayo, "Caught Between Roadblocks, They Were Sitting Ducks for Boko Haram Massacre," CNN, February 15, 2020, https://www.cnn.com/2020/02/15/africa/nigeria-boko -haram-fire-auno-intl/index.html.

3. Haleem Olatunji, "Zulum Shouts at Army Commander over Fresh Boko Haram Attack," TheCable, February 10, 2020, https://www.thecable.ng/zulum-shouts-at-army-commander-over-fresh-boko-haram-attack.

4. Mr Integrity (@Integrity56), "How do you lock the city gate, leaving innocent citizens to sleep on the Highway in a conflict zone, without providing adequate protection for them? What kind of a Country is this?" Twitter, February 11, 2020, 7:23 a.m., https://twitter.com/Intergrity56/status/1227221591777521664.

5. Jideofor Adibe, "Explaining the Emergence of Boko Haram," Brookings, May 6, 2014, https://www.brookings.edu/blog/africa-in-focus/2014/05/06/explaining-the-emergence-of-boko-haram/.

6. Virginia Comolli, "Boko Haram and Islamic State," in *Jihadism Transformed: Al-Qaeda and Islamic State's Global Battle of Ideas*, eds. Simon Staffell and Akil Awan (New York: Oxford University Press, 2016), 129; Oxford Scholarship Online, https://www.oxfordscholarship.com/view/10.1093/acprof:oso/9780190650292.001.0001/acprof-9780190650292.

7. Scott MacEachern, *Searching for Boko Haram: A History of Violence in Central Africa* (New York: Oxford University Press, 2018), 2.

8. MacEachern, *Searching for Boko Haram*, 5.

9. MacEachern, 5–6.

10. MacEachern, 6.

11. Lamin O. Sanneh, *Beyond Jihad: The Pacifist Tradition in West African Islam* (New York: Oxford University Press, 2016), 259.

12. Sanneh, *Beyond Jihad*, 261.

13. Sanneh, 263.

14. MacEachern, *Searching for Boko Haram*, 7–8.

15. MacEachern, 6–7.

16. Daniel E. Agbiboa, "Sharia and the Nigerian Constitution: Strange Bedfellows?," ConstitutionNet, April 16, 2015, http://constitutionnet.org/news/sharia-and-nigerian-constitution-strange-bedfellows.

17. Alexander Thurston, *Boko Haram: The History of an African Jihadist Movement* (Princeton, NJ: Princeton University Press, 2019), 13.

18. "Boko Haram Leader, Shekau, Threatens to Attack Buhari, Lists Condition for Chibok Girls' Release," Sahara Reporters, February 13, 2020, http://saharareporters.com/2020/02/13 /boko-haram-leader-shekau-threatens-attack-buhari-lists -condition-chibok-girls%E2%80%99-release.

19. Thurston, *Boko Haram*, 287.

20. David Cook, "Boko Haram Escalates Attacks on Christians in Northern Nigeria," *CTC Sentinel* 5, no. 4 (April 2012): 8, https:// ctc.usma.edu/boko-haram-escalates-attacks-on-christians-in -northern-nigeria/.

21. Abubakar Shekau, quoted in Thurston, *Boko Haram*, 159.

22. Abubakar Shekau, quoted in Jideofor Adibe, "How Boko Haram Went from a Peaceful Islamic Sect to One of the World's Deadliest Terrorists in a Decade," Quartz Africa, November 14, 2019, https://qz.com/africa/1748873/boko -harams-10-year-reign-in-nigeria-has-been-devastating/.

23. Thurston, *Boko Haram*, 176.

24. Claire Felter, Jonathan Masters, and Mohammed Aly Sergie, "Al-Shabab," Council on Foreign Relations, last modified January 10, 2020, https://www.cfr.org/backgrounder/al-shabab.

25. Felter, Masters, and Sergie, "Al-Shabab."

26. Felter, Masters, and Sergie, "Al-Shabab."

27. Mapping Militant Organizations, "Al Shabaab," Stanford Center for International Security and Cooperation, last updated January 2019, https://cisac.fsi.stanford.edu/mappingmilitants/profiles /al-shabaab.

28. Felter, Masters, and Sergie, "Al-Shabab."

29. Mary Harper, *Everything You Have Told Me Is True: The Many Faces of Al Shabaab* (London: Hurst & Company, 2019), 3.

30. Felter, Masters, and Sergie, "Al-Shabab."

31. Daniel Howden, "Terror in Nairobi: The Full Story Behind

Al-Shabaab's Mall Attack," *Guardian*, October 4, 2013, https://www.theguardian.com/world/2013/oct/04/westgate-mall-attacks-kenya.

32. "Garissa University College Attack in Kenya: What Happened?," BBC News, June 19, 2019, https://www.bbc.com/news/world-africa-48621924.

33. Anugrah Kumar, "Al-Shabaab Warns All Christians to Leave Northeastern Kenya," *Christian Post*, March 2, 2020, https://www.christianpost.com/news/al-shabaab-warns-all-christians-to-leave-northeastern-kenya.html.

34. Ali Dhere, quoted in Kumar, "Al-Shabaab Warns All Christians."

35. Kumar, "Al-Shabaab Warns All Christians."

36. Harper, *Everything You Have Told Me*, 4.

37. Dina Temple-Raston, "New Charges in Somali Terror Case," NPR, November 23, 2009, https://www.npr.org/templates/story/story.php?storyId=120709855.

Chapter 2: The Strategy

1. Terrence McCoy, "Paying for Terrorism: Where Does Boko Haram Gets Its Money From?," *Independent*, June 6, 2014, https://www.independent.co.uk/news/world/africa/paying-for-terrorism-where-does-boko-haram-gets-its-money-from-9503948.html.

2. Catherine Soi, "Nigeria: Boko Haram Exploiting Poor Children for Suicide Attacks," Al Jazeera, September 8, 2017, https://www.aljazeera.com/video/news/2017/09/nigeria-boko-haram-increasingly-exploiting-poor-children-suicide-attacks-170908055347924.html.

3. "Use of Children as 'Human Bombs' Rising in North East Nigeria," UNICEF, August 22, 2017, https://www.unicef.org/press-releases/use-of-children-human-bombs-rising-north-east-nigeria.

4. Carley Petesch, "Boko Haram Leaves 3 Million Kids Out of School in N. Nigeria," Associated Press, September 29, 2017,

https://apnews.com/63a58b77201e47cfb54f17ec73260cf8
/Boko-Haram-leaves-3-million-kids-out-of-school-in-N.-Nigeria.

5. Petesch, "Boko Haram Leaves 3 Million Kids Out of School."

6. Reuters, "Hundreds of Chained Men and Boys Are Rescued in Nigeria," *New York Times*, September 27, 2019, https://www .nytimes.com/2019/09/27/world/africa/nigeria-boys-torture -slavery.html.

7. Prinesha Naidoo, "Nigeria Tops South Africa as the Continent's Biggest Economy," Bloomberg, published March 3, 2020; updated March 4, 2020, https://www.bloomberg.com/news/articles/2020 -03-03/nigeria-now-tops-south-africa-as-the-continent-s -biggest-economy.

8. "Oil Reserves by Country," Worldometer, accessed May 24, 2020, https://www.worldometers.info/oil/oil-reserves-by-country/.

9. "African Countries by Population (2020)," Worldometer, accessed May 24, 2020, https://www.worldometers.info /population/countries-in-africa-by-population/.

10. "World Poverty Clock," World Data Lab, accessed May 24, 2020, https://worldpoverty.io/map.

11. Emele Onu et al., "Six People Fall into Extreme Poverty in This Nation Every Minute," Bloomberg, February 21, 2019, https://www.bloomberg.com/news/articles/2019-02-22 /six-people-fall-into-extreme-poverty-in-this-nation-every -minute.

12. Peter Beaumont and Isaac Abrak, "Oil-Rich Nigeria Outstrips India as Country with Most People in Poverty," *Guardian*, July 16, 2018, https://www.theguardian.com/global-development /2018/jul/16/oil-rich-nigeria-outstrips-india-most-people-in -poverty.

13. "World Poverty Clock."

14. Marc-Olivier Cantin, "Reexamining the Terrorism -Poverty Nexus," *Journal of International Affairs*, April 29, 2018, https://jia.sipa.columbia.edu/online-articles/reexamining -terrorism-poverty-nexus.

15. UNDP, "Journey to Extremism in Africa: Drivers, Incentives, and the Tipping Point for Recruitment" (New York: United Nations Development Programme, 2017), 6; http://journey-to -extremism.undp.org/en/reports.

16. UNDP, "Journey to Extremism in Africa," 58.

17. Beaumont and Abrak, "Oil-Rich Nigeria Outstrips India."

18. Soi, "Boko Haram Exploiting Poor Children."

19. Lucie Sarr, "Christian, Muslim Leaders in Nigeria Commit Themselves to Peace," La Croix International, February 25, 2020, https://international.la-croix.com/news/christian-muslim -leaders-in-nigeria-commit-themselves-to-peace/11879.

20. Soi, "Boko Haram Exploiting Poor Children."

21. Soi, "Boko Haram Exploiting Poor Children."

22. Steven Brooke, "The Muslim Brotherhood's Social Outreach After the Egyptian Coup," Brookings, August 2015, https://www .brookings.edu/wp-content/uploads/2016/07/Egypt_Brooke -FINALE.pdf.

23. Marie Vannetzel, "The Muslim Brotherhood's 'Virtuous Society' and State Developmentalism in Egypt: The Politics of 'Goodness,'" International Development Policy 8 (2017), https:// doi.org/10.4000/poldev.2327.

24. Vannetzel, "Muslim Brotherhood's 'Virtuous Society.'"

25. Cantin, "Reexamining the Terrorism-Poverty Nexus."

26. Jideofor Adibe, "Explaining the Emergence of Boko Haram," Brookings, May 6, 2014, https://www.brookings .edu/blog/africa-in-focus/2014/05/06/explaining-the -emergence-of-boko-haram/.

27. Élodie Apard, "The Words of Boko Haram: Understanding Speeches by Momammed Yusaf and Abubakar Shekau," Afrique Contemporaine 255, no. 3 (2015): 41–69, https://www.cairn-int .info/article-E_AFCO_255_0043--the-words-of-boko-haram .htm#.

28. Mohammed Yusuf, quoted in Apard, "Words of Boko Haram."

29. Abubakar Shekau, quoted in Atta Barkindo, "Abubakr Shekau:

Boko Haram's Underestimated Corporatist-Strategic Leader," in *Boko Haram Beyond the Headlines: Analyses of Africa's Enduring Insurgency*, ed. Jacob Zenn (West Point, NY: Combating Terrorism Center at West Point, May 2018), 58.

30. Apard, "Words of Boko Haram."

31. John Campbell, "Nigerian Government Has Been Negotiating with Boko Haram for 'Some Time,'" Council on Foreign Relations, March 28, 2018, https://www.cfr.org/blog/nigerian-government-has-been-negotiating-boko-haram-some-time.

32. "Nigeria's Boko Haram 'Got $3m Ransom' to Free Hostages," BBC News, April 27, 2013, https://www.bbc.com/news/world-africa-22320077.

33. "Nigeria: Sultan of Sokoto Condemns Boko Haram Crackdown," BBC News, July 29, 2011, https://www.bbc.com/news/world-africa-14342863.

34. "Sultan Abubakar Gives Stunning Insight into Boko Haram Emergence," PM News, February 21, 2020, https://www.pmnewsnigeria.com/2020/02/21/sultan-abubakar-gives-stunning-insight-into-boko-haram-emergence/.

35. Johannes Harnischfeger, "Islamisation and Ethnic Conversion in Nigeria," *Anthropos* 101, no. 1 (2006): 37–53, https://www.jstor.org/stable/40466619.

36. Harnischfeger, "Islamisation and Ethnic Conversion in Nigeria," 38.

37. Muhammadu Buhari, "Buhari: Pastor Andimi's Faith Should Inspire All Nigerians," *Christianity Today*, February 3, 2020, https://www.christianitytoday.com/ct/2020/february-web-only/nigeria-president-buhari-pastor-lawan-andimi-boko-haram.html.

38. "Nigeria's Politics Has Nothing to Do with Religion, Says Jonathan," *Vanguard*, January 14, 2015, https://www.vanguardngr.com/2015/01/nigerias-politics-nothing-religion-says-jonathan/; Ameh Comrade Godwin, "Boko Haram Is a Fraud, It Has Nothing to Do with Religion —Buhari," *Daily Post*, April 28, 2015, https://dailypost.ng/2015/04/28/boko-haram-is-a-fraud-it-has-nothing-to-do-with-religion-buhari/.

39. "Nigeria: 'Our Job Is to Shoot, Slaughter and Kill'—Boko Haram's Reign of Terror in North-East Nigeria," AllAfrica, April 14, 2015, https://allafrica.com/stories/201504132730 .html.

40. Samson Toromade, "President Paid Boko Haram €3m for 103 Chibok Girls," Pulse Nigeria, December 25, 2017, https://www .pulse.ng/news/local/buhari-president-paid-boko-haram -euro3m-for-103-chibok-girls/jt3fdp0.

41. "Corruption in Nigeria Survey Reveals Far-Reaching Impact," United Nations: Office on Drugs and Crime, August 21, 2017, https://www.unodc.org/unodc/en/frontpage/2017/August /corruption-in-nigeria-survey-reveals-far-reaching-impact.html.

42. Julia Zorthian, "President Buhari Says Nigeria Has 'Technically' Beaten Boko Haram," *Time*, December 24, 2015, https://time .com/4161175/buhari-nigeria-technically-won-war-boko-haram/.

43. "The Many 'Defeats' of Boko Haram," Africa Check, September 26, 2017, https://africacheck.org/spot-check/13663/.

44. Samson Toromade, "Buhari Needs to Be More Honest About Boko Haram's 'Defeat,'" Pulse Nigeria, January 2, 2018, https://www.pulse.ng/news/local/pulse-opinion-buhari -needs-to-be-more-honest-about-boko-harams-defeat /y3xwlnl.

45. Dennis Erezi, "Boko Haram Now 'Substantially' Defeated, Says Buhari," *Guardian*, October 16, 2019, https://guardian.ng/news /boko-haram-now-substantially-defeated-says-buhari/.

46. Guillaume Lavallée, "Nigeria Insists Boko Haram 'Defeated' After 10-Year Insurgency," Rappler, July 31, 2019, https:// www.rappler.com/world/regions/africa/236796-nigeria-insists -boko-haram-defeated-july-30-2019.

47. "Boko Haram Leader, Shekau, Threatens to Attack Buhari, Lists Condition for Chibok Girls' Release," Sahara Reporters, February 13, 2020, http://saharareporters.com/2020/02/13 /boko-haram-leader-shekau-threatens-attack-buhari-lists -condition-chibok-girls%E2%80%99-release.

Chapter 3: Criminal Bandits or Jihadi Terrorists?

1. Don Bosco Onyalla, "Four Seminarians Abducted in Nigeria," Catholic News Agency, January 13, 2020, https://www .catholicnewsagency.com/news/four-seminarians-abducted -in-nigeria-88125.

2. Ben Agande, "Bandits Abducts Four 'Seminarians' in Kaduna Catholic School," *Vanguard*, January 9, 2020, https://www .vanguardngr.com/2020/01/bandits-abducts-four-seminarians -in-kaduna-catholic-school/.

3. John Gabriel, "Missing Student of Good Shepherd Seminary Found Dead in Kaduna," *Daily Post*, February 2, 2020, https:// dailypost.ng/2020/02/02/missing-student-of-good-shepherd -seminary-found-dead-in-kaduna/.

4. Gabriel, "Missing Student."

5. "Seminarian's Killing a 'Defining Moment' for Christians in Nigeria," Catholic News Agency, February 11, 2020, https://www .catholicnewsagency.com/news/seminarians-killing-a-defining -moment-for-christians-in-nigeria-80610.

6. "Kidnappers Killed Nnadi After Getting Ransom, I Pray God Forgives Them—Raphael, Twin Brother of Slain Kaduna Seminarian," *Punch*, February 8, 2020, https://punchng.com /kidnappers-killed-nnadi-after-getting-ransom-i-pray-god -forgives-them-raphael-twin-brother-of-slain-kaduna -seminarian/.

7. Molly Kilete, "Exclusive: Why We Killed Kaduna Catholic Seminarian—Kidnap Leader Confesses," *Daily Sun*, April 30, 2020, https://www.sunnewsonline.com/exclusive-why-we-killed -kaduna-catholic-seminarian-kidnap-leader-confesses/.

8. Kilete, "Why We Killed Kaduna Catholic Seminarian."

9. Maria Lozano, adapted by Amanda Bridget Griffin, "Four Seminarians Abducted—Nigeria at Risk of Becoming a Failed State," ACN Canada, January 13, 2020, https://acn-canada.org /acn-news-four-seminarians-abducted-nigeria/.

10. Lozano, "Four Seminarians Abducted."

11. Toyin Falola and Matthew M. Heaton, *A History of Nigeria* (Cambridge: Cambridge University Press, 2008), 62.

12. Falola and Heaton, *History of Nigeria*, 71.

13. Bernard-Henri Lévy, "The New War Against Africa's Christians," *Wall Street Journal*, December 20, 2019, https://www.wsj.com /articles/the-new-war-against-africas-christians-11576880200.

14. Samuel Smith, "At Least 50 Nigerian Christians Killed by Fulani Attacks in March, NGO Reports," *Christian Post*, April 7, 2020, https://www.christianpost.com/news/at-least-50-nigerian -christians-killed-by-fulani-attacks-in-march-ngo-reports.html.

15. Sam Olukoya, "Report: 86 Killed in Nigeria as Farmers, Herders Clash," Associated Press, June 25, 2018, https://apnews .com/955e029b44b9429d9f6993024a1d7b66.

16. Ciara Nugent, "How Climate Change Is Spurring Land Conflict in Nigeria," *Time*, June 28, 2018, https://time.com/5324712 /climate-change-nigeria/.

17. Stephanie Busari, "Nigeria: Scores Killed, Homes Burned in Plateau State Attacks," CNN, June 25, 2018, https://www.cnn .com/2018/06/25/africa/nigeria-attacks-intl/index.html.

18. John Campbell, "Conflict in Nigeria Is More Complicated Than 'Christians vs. Muslims,'" Council on Foreign Relations, May 1, 2019, https://www.cfr.org/blog/conflict-nigeria-more -complicated-christians-vs-muslims.

19. *U.S. Policy Toward Nigeria: West Africa's Troubled Titan: Hearing Before the Subcommittee on Africa, Global Health, and Human Rights of the Committee on Foreign Affairs*, 112th Cong. 2 (2012), 5, https://www.govinfo.gov/content/pkg/CHRG-112hhrg74961 /html/CHRG-112hhrg74961.htm.

20. *U.S. Policy Toward Nigeria*, 5

21. Nina Shea, "The Obama State Department's Understanding of Boko Haram Was Even More Delusional Than You Thought," Hudson Institute, May 9, 2014, https://www.hudson.org /research/10284-the-obama-state-department-s-understanding -of-boko-haram-was-even-more-delusional-than-you-thought.

22. Shea, "Obama State Department's Understanding of Boko Haram."

23. Shea, "Obama State Department's Understanding of Boko Haram."

24. Michael R. Gordon, "Schoolgirl Abductions Put Scrutiny on U.S. Terrorism Strategy," *New York Times*, May 8, 2014, https://www.nytimes.com/2014/05/09/world/africa/schoolgirl-abductions-put-scrutiny-on-us-terrorism-strategy.html.

25. Gordon, "Schoolgirl Abductions."

26. Gordon, "Schoolgirl Abductions."

27. Naziru Mikailu, "Making Sense of Nigeria's Fulani-Farmer Conflict," BBC News, May 5, 2016, https://www.bbc.com/news/world-africa-36139388.

28. Boukary Sangare, "Fulani People and Jihadism in Sahel and West African Countries," Foundation for Strategic Research, February 8, 2019, https://www.frstrategie.org/en/programs/observatoire-du-monde-arabo-musulman-et-du-sahel/fulani-people-and-jihadism-sahel-and-west-african-countries-2019.

29. "Nigeria Attacks: Mosque Bomb Blasts Kill Dozens in Mubi," BBC News, May 1, 2018, https://www.bbc.com/news/world-africa-43967738.

30. "'Boko Haram' Gunmen Kill Senior Muslim Cleric in Northeast Nigeria," Zee News, updated May 31, 2014, https://zeenews.india.com/news/world/boko-haram-gunmen-kill-senior-muslim-cleric-in-northeast-nigeria_936178.html.

31. Samuel Ogundipe, "Military, Police Complicit in Killings Across Nigeria—T.Y. Danjuma," Premium Times, March 24, 2018, https://www.premiumtimesng.com/news/headlines/262959-military-police-complicit-in-killings-across-nigeria-t-y-danjuma.html.

32. Bukola Adebayo, "Muslim Cleric Who Hid Christians During Attacks Honored in the US," CNN, July 18, 2019, https://www.cnn.com/2019/07/18/africa/nigeria-cleric-honored-intl/index.html.

33. "International Religious Freedom Award Winners," US Department of State, July 17, 2019, https://www.state.gov /international-religious-freedom-award-winners/.

34. "International Religious Freedom Award Winners," US Department of State.

35. Fikayo Olowolagba, "Anarchy May Arise—Archbishop Martins Laments Murder of 18-Year-Old Catholic Seminarian by Kidnappers," *Daily Post*, February 3, 2020, https://dailypost .ng/2020/02/03/anarchy-may-arise-archbishop-martins-laments -murder-of-18-year-old-catholic-seminarian-by-kidnappers/.

36. Lévy, "The New War Against Africa's Christians."

37. Lévy, "The New War Against Africa's Christians."

Chapter 4: An Improbable Journey to Faith and Freedom

1. Religious Literacy Project, "The Transatlantic Slave Trade," Harvard Divinity School, accessed May 24, 2020, https://rlp.hds .harvard.edu/faq/transatlantic-slave-trade-nigeria.

2. Religious Literacy Project, "Transatlantic Slave Trade."

3. Andrew F. Walls, "Crowther, Samuel Adjai [or Ajayi] (c. 1807– 1891)," in *Biographical Dictionary of Christian Missions*, ed. Gerald H. Anderson (New York: Macmillan Reference, 1998), reprinted by Boston University School of Theology, https://www .bu.edu/missiology/missionary-biography/c-d/crowther-samuel -adjai-or-ajayi-c-1807-1891/.

4. Walls, "Crowther, Samuel Adjai."

5. Takim Williams, "#InContext: William Wilberforce," The Human Trafficking Institute, July 11, 2017, https://www .traffickinginstitute.org/incontext-william-wilberforce/.

6. Religious Literacy Project, "Transatlantic Slave Trade."

7. Omar Alleyne-Lawler, "Community Heroes of the Past: Bishop Samuel Ajayi Crowther," Black History 365, August 25, 2015, https://www.blackhistorymonth.org.uk/article/section/history -of-slavery/community-heroes-of-the-past-bishop-samuel -ajayi-crowther/.

8. Religious Literacy Project, "Transatlantic Slave Trade."

9. Ayodeji Abodunde, *A Heritage of Faith: A History of Christianity in Nigeria* (Lagos: Pierce Watershed, 2018), 38–39.

10. Abodunde, *Heritage of Faith*, 38–39.

11. Abodunde, 42–43.

12. Abodunde, 45.

13. Abodunde, 46.

14. Abodunde, 47–48.

15. Abodunde, 58.

16. "Nigeria Chibok Abductions: What We Know," BBC News, May 8, 2017, https://www.bbc.com/news/world-africa-32299943.

17. Helon Habila, *The Chibok Girls: The Boko Haram Kidnappings & Islamic Militancy in Nigeria* (London: Penguin Books, 2017), 32–35.

18. Johnnie Moore, *The Martyr's Oath: Living for the Jesus They're Willing to Die For* (Carol Stream, IL: Tyndale House, 2017), 7–9.

19. Habila, *Chibok Girls*, 32–35.

20. Tulip Mazumdar, "Chibok Girls 'Forced to Join Nigeria's Boko Haram,'" BBC News, June 29, 2015, https://www.bbc.com/news/world-africa-33259003.

21. Mazumdar, "Chibok Girls."

22. Mazumdar, "Chibok Girls."

23. Habila, *Chibok Girls*, 32–35.

24. Habila, 32–35.

25. Mazumdar, "Chibok Girls."

26. Felix Onuah, "Nigeria Says 110 Girls Unaccounted for After Boko Haram Attack," Reuters, February 25, 2018, https://www.reuters.com/article/us-nigeria-security/nigeria-says-110-girls-unaccounted-for-after-boko-haram-attack-idUSKCN1G90Q3.

27. Onuah, "Nigeria Says 110 Girls Unaccounted For."

28. Onuah, "Nigeria Says 110 Girls Unaccounted For."

29. Adelani Adepegba, "FG Paid Huge Ransom for Release of Dapchi Girls—UN Report," *Punch*, August 16, 2018, https://punchng.com/fg-paid-huge-ransom-for-release-of-dapchi-girls-un-report/.

30. Chika Oduah, "Dapchi Girls' Release Could Stir Up Religious Tensions in Nigeria," Voice of America, March 23, 2018, https://www.voanews.com/africa/dapchi-girls-release-could-stir-religious-tensions-nigeria.

31. Ruth Maclean, "Boko Haram Kept One Dapchi Girl Who Refused to Deny Her Christianity," *Guardian*, March 24, 2018, https://www.theguardian.com/world/2018/mar/24/boko-haram-kept-one-dapchi-nigeria-girl-who-refused-to-deny-her-christianity.

32. Maclean, "Boko Haram."

33. Maclean, "Boko Haram."

34. "Nigeria: Again, Buhari Restates Commitment to Free Leah Sharibu, Other Boko Haram Captives," AllAfrica, February 18, 2020, https://allafrica.com/stories/202002190049.html.

35. Joe Parkinson and Gbenga Akingbule, "Six Years After #BringBackOurGirls, Freed Chibok Captives Face Fresh Danger," *Wall Street Journal*, April 14, 2020, https://www.wsj.com/articles/six-years-after-bringbackourgirls-freed-chibok-captives-face-fresh-danger-11586862002.

36. John H. Darch, *Missionary Imperialists?: Missionaries, Government and the Growth of the British Empire in the Tropics, 1860–1885* (Eugene, OR: Wipf & Stock Publishers, 2009), 177–78.

Chapter 5: Lawless

1. Carol Glatz, "Pope Francis: Priests Should Be 'Shepherds Living with the Smell of the Sheep,'" *Catholic Telegraph*, March 28, 2013, https://www.thecatholictelegraph.com/pope-francis-priests-should-be-shepherds-living-with-the-smell-of-the-sheep/13439.

2. Mishnah Sanhedrin 4:5.

3. Neil Munshi, "Threat of Abduction Makes Nigeria a High-Risk Business," *Financial Times*, November 21, 2019, https://www.ft.com/content/99d6aaea-e394-11e9-9743-db5a370481bc.

4. "Nigerian Police Battle a Growing Kidnapping Crisis," Al Jazeera, August 24, 2019, https://www.aljazeera.com /news/2019/08/nigerian-police-battle-growing-kidnapping -crisis-190824124410317.html.

5. Orji Sunday, "Nigeria's Kidnapping Cartels Thrive in the Absence of Governance," TRT World, September 5, 2019, https:// www.trtworld.com/magazine/nigeria-s-kidnapping-cartels -thrive-in-the-absence-of-governance-29562.

6. Sunday, "Nigeria's Kidnapping Cartels."

7. Jamilah Nasir, "Revealed: Doctor Who Lost Wife to Kidnappers Donated Police Station to His Community," TheCable, February 2, 2020, https://www.thecable.ng/revealed-doctor-who-lost-wife -to-kidnappers-donated-police-station-to-his-community.

8. Nasir, "Doctor Who Lost Wife to Kidnappers."

9. "Gunmen Kill Doctor's Wife Abducted in Kaduna, 'Demand N20m' for Release of Her Children," TheCable, February 1, 2020, https://www.thecable.ng/breaking-gunmen-kill-doctors -wife-abducted-in-kaduna-demand-n20m-for-release-of-her -children.

10. "Gunmen Kill Doctor's Wife," TheCable.

11. Seyi Gesinde, "Kidnappers Free Two Children of Kaduna Doctor, Philip Ataga, After Killing Wife," *Nigerian Tribune*, February 7, 2020, https://tribuneonlineng.com/kidnappers-free-two -children-of-kaduna-doctor-philip-ataga-after-killing-wife/.

12. "Couple Abducted from Wedding in Attacks in Northwest Nigeria That Kill 12 Christians," Morning Star News, April 29, 2020, https://morningstarnews.org/2020/04/couple-abducted -from-wedding-in-attacks-in-northwest-nigeria-that-kill-12 -christians/.

13. "12 Christians Killed, Couple Kidnapped from Church During Wedding in Nigeria," *Christian Post*, May 2, 2020, https://www.christianpost.com/news/12-christians-killed -couple-kidnapped-from-church-during-wedding-in-nigeria .html.

14. Samuel Smith, "Over 20 Killed in Spate of New Fulani Massacres on Nigerian Christians," *Christian Post*, May 14, 2020, https://www.christianpost.com/news/over-20-killed-in-spate-of-new-fulani-massacres-on-nigerian-christians.html.

15. Smith, "Over 20 Killed."

16. Douglas Burton, "Cell Phone Raises Questions of Links Between Jihadis and Nigeria's Police and Army," Zenger, April 23, 2020, https://zenger.news/2020/04/23/cell-phone-raises-questions-of-links-between-attackers-and-nigeria-authorities/.

17. Burton, "Cell Phone."

18. Burton, "Cell Phone."

19. Burton, "Cell Phone."

20. Internal report provided to us by an NGO.

21. Internal report provided to us by an NGO.

22. Internal report provided to us by an NGO.

23. Isa Abdulsalami Ahovi, Joseph Wantu, and Owen Akenzua, "Protest as Herdsmen Kill over 25 in Plateau, Delta," *Guardian*, October 17, 2017, https://guardian.ng/news/protest-as-herdsmen-kill-over-25-in-plateau-delta/.

24. "Summary of Judgment of the ECOWAS Court in the Case of Rev. Fr. Solomon MFA & 11 ORS. v. Federal Republic of Nigeria Suit No.: ECW/CCJ/APP/11/16," Nigerian Catholic Reporter, March 4, 2019, https://nigeriancatholicreporter.com/summary-of-judgment-of-the-ecowas-court-in-the-case-of-rev-fr-solomon-mfa-11-ors-v-federal-republic-of-nigeria-suit-no-ecw-ccj-app-11-16/.

25. Terhemba Daka, "Buhari Meets Miyetti Allah in Aso Rock," *Guardian*, January 19, 2019, https://guardian.ng/news/buhari-meets-miyetti-allah-in-aso-rock/.

26. "Kidnappings: Ban Miyetti Allah, CAN Tells Buhari," Sahara Reporters, September 1, 2019, http://saharareporters.com/2019/09/01/kidnappings-ban-miyetti-allah-can-tells-buhari.

Chapter 6: Down but Not Out

1. Nathan Morley, "IS Militants Behead 11 Christians in Nigeria on Christmas Day," Vatican News, December 27, 2019, https://www .vaticannews.va/en/world/news/2019-12/islamic-state-nigeria -christians-killed-on-christmas.html.

2. "Nigeria: Child Terrorist Executes Christian Student," Independent Catholic News, January 23, 2020, https://www .indcatholicnews.com/news/38777.

3. "Child Terrorist," Independent Catholic News.

4. Johnnie Moore, *Defying ISIS: Preserving Christianity in the Place of Its Birth and in Your Own Backyard* (Nashville: Thomas Nelson, 2015), 36–38.

5. "Pastor's Wife Killed by Abductors in Kaduna State," CSW, October 3, 2019, https://www.csw.org.uk/2019/10/03/press/4472/article.htm.

6. "Boko Haram Executes Two Christian Aid Workers in Nigeria," Morning Star News, September 30, 2019, https:// morningstarnews.org/2019/09/boko-haram-executes-two -christian-aid-workers-in-nigeria/.

7. "Boko Haram Executes Two Christian Aid Workers," Morning Star News.

8. "Pastor's Wife Killed," CSW.

9. "Pastor's Wife Killed," CSW.

10. "Christians 'Appalled' after Pregnant Pastor's Wife Kidnapped and Killed in Nigeria," Christian Today, October 3, 2019, https:// christiantoday.com/article/christians-appalled-after-pregnant -pastors-wife-kidnapped-and-killed-in-nigeria/133353.htm.

11. John Shiklam, "Nigeria: Bandits Kill Pastor's Wife After Collecting Ransom in Kaduna," AllAfrica, September 25, 2019, https://allafrica.com/stories/201909250733.html.

12. Alexis Akwagyiram, "Mercy Corps Suspends Northeast Nigeria Work After Army Shuts Offices," Reuters, September 25, 2019, https://www.reuters.com/article/us-nigeria-security /mercy-corps-suspends-northeast-nigeria-work-after-army -shuts-offices-idUSKBN1WB04B.

13. "Mercy Corps Is Extremely Concerned About Ongoing Closures in Northeast Nigeria," Mercy Corps news release, Reliefweb, October 25, 2019, https://reliefweb.int/report/nigeria /mercy-corps-extremely-concerned-about-ongoing-closures -northeast-nigeria.

14. Yomi Kazeem, "Nigeria's Military Is in a Battle with Humanitarian NGOs in the Country's Troubled Northeast," Quartz Africa, September 26, 2019, https://qz.com/africa /1716064/nigerian-army-shuts-mercy-corps-ngos-amid-boko -haram-crisis/.

15. Ahmad Salkida (@A_Salkida), "The group, in a horrific video of the execution, said it took the action because 'the government deceived them'," Twitter, September 25, 2019, 2:02 a.m., https:// twitter.com/A_Salkida/status/1176753867603755008.

16. Morning Star News, "Two Nigerian Evangelicals Executed in Boko Haram Video," *Christianity Today*, October 1, 2019, https:// www.christianitytoday.com/news/2019/october/two-nigerian -evangelicals-executed-in-boko-haram-video.html.

17. "Nigerian Brethren District Leader and Ecumenical Leader Lawan Andimi Has Been Executed by Boko Haram," Church of the Brethren, January 21, 2020, http://www.brethren.org/news /2020/nigerian-brethren-leader-executed.html.

18. "Nigerian Brethren District Leader," Church of the Brethren.

19. "Boko Haram Executes Chair of Christian Association of Nigeria in Adamawa State," CSW, January 21, 2020, https://www.csw.org .uk/2020/01/21/press/4530/article.htm.

20. Jayson Casper, "Boko Haram Executes Pastor Who Turned Hostage Video into Testimony," *Christianity Today*, January 21, 2020, https://www.christianitytoday.com/news/2020/january /nigeria-boko-haram-kidnapped-pastor-hostage-video -testimony.html.

21. "Conference Marking the Second Year Anniversary of Leah Sharibu in Captivity," Dunamis.TV, streamed live on February

19, 2020, YouTube video, 11:20/1:34:07, https://www.youtube
.com/watch?v=q8Ma7pqOOsA&feature=youtu.be.

Chapter 7: Thousands of Names

1. Johnnie Moore, *The Martyr's Oath: Living for the Jesus They're Willing to Die For* (Carol Stream, IL: Tyndale House, 2017), 2.
2. Moore, *Martyr's Oath*, 4.
3. Moore, 5–6.
4. ICON and PSJ, *Nigeria's Silent Slaughter: Genocide in Nigeria and the Implications for the International Community* (Nigeria: International Committee on Nigeria and International Organization for Peace Building and Social Justice, 2020), 136–37.
5. ICON and PSJ, *Nigeria's Silent Slaughter*, 137.
6. "Irigwe Genocide: The Slaughter of a People," April 21, 2020, Religious Freedom and Global Security News, newsletter, International Committee on Nigeria, https://standwithnigeria .org/resources/news/.
7. Agabus Pwanagba, "Plateau Attacks: 327 Killed, 14,968 Displaced in Irigwe Land—Report," *Daily Post*, January 9, 2020, https:// dailypost.ng/2020/01/09/plateau-attacks-327-killed-14968 -displaced-in-irigwe-land-report/.
8. Carma Henry, "'The Government Is Silent': Muslim Tribesmen Kill Christian Pastor and Burn Down School in Nigerian Village," *Westside Gazette*, April 15, 2020, https:// thewestsidegazette.com/the-government-is-silent-muslim -tribesmen-kill-christian-pastor-and-burn-down-school-in -nigerian-village/.
9. Pastor Yakubu Kpasha, quoted in Henry, "Government Is Silent."
10. Ben Kwashi, letter to the International Committee on Nigeria, February 27, 2020.
11. Baroness Caroline Cox, "UK Government 'Turning a Deaf Ear' to Genocide in Nigeria," Christian Solidarity International: Nigeria Report, accessed May 24, 2020, https://www.nigeria -report.org/commentaries/baroness-cox/.

12. Baroness Caroline Cox, letter to International Organization for Peace Building and Social Justice, November 24, 2019.

13. James Bennet, "Clinton Declares U.S. and the World Failed Rwandans," *New York Times*, March 26, 1998, https://archive .nytimes.com/www.nytimes.com/library/world/032698clinton -africa.html.

14. Quoted in Abraham Cooper, "From Sudan to North Korea and Syria: A Plea to President Obama to Activate His Atrocities Prevention Board," *Algemeiner*, May 22, 2013, https://www .algemeiner.com/2013/05/22/from-sudan-to-north-korea-and-syria -a-plea-to-president-obama-to-activate-his-atrocities-prevention -board/.

15. "Ese Oruru: Abducted, Raped, Impregnated Teenager Yet to Get Justice 4 Years Later," Sahara Reporters, November 7, 2019, http:// saharareporters.com/2019/11/07/ese-oruru-abducted-raped -impregnated-teenager-yet-get-justice-4-years-later.

16. John Campbell, "Lamido Sanusi: A Man of Nigeria's Past and Possibly Its Future," Council on Foreign Relations, March 31, 2020, https://www.cfr.org/blog/lamido-sanusi-man-nigerias -past-and-possibly-its-future.

17. "Abduction: 14-Yr-Old Ese Oruru 5 Months Pregnant," *Vanguard*, March 3, 2016, https://www.vanguardngr.com/2016/03/abduction -14-yr-old-ese-oruru-5-months-pregnant/.

18. Kunle Awosiyan, "Ese Oruru: Emir Sanusi Explains His Role," SilverbirdTV, March 1, 2016, https://silverbirdtv.com /uncategorized/25378/ese-oruru-emir-sanusi-explains-his-role/.

19. "Abduction," *Vanguard*.

20. "Nobody Should Steal a Christian Girl and Marry Her—CAN Secretary, Asake," *Punch*, March 6, 2016, https://punchng.com /nobody-should-steal-a-christian-girl-and-marry-her-can -secretary-asake/.

21. "Nobody Should Steal a Christian Girl," *Punch*.

22. "Ese Oruru," Sahara Reporters.

23. Onungwe Obe, "Nigeria: Finally, Court Sentences Ese Oruru's

Abductor to 26 Years," AllAfrica, May 22, 2020, https://allafrica
.com/stories/202005220470.html.

24. "Ese Oruru: Bashir Ahmed Promises Twitter User to Influence
Yunusa Dahiru's Court Conviction," Sahara Reporters, May 22,
2020, http://saharareporters.com/2020/05/22/ese-oruru
-bashir-ahmed-promises-twitter-user-influence-yunusa
-dahirus-court-conviction.

25. "I Hold Yunusa Innocent Until I Hear from Him—Sheikh
Ahmad," *Punch*, March 5, 2016, https://punchng.com/i-hold
-yunusa-innocent-until-i-hear-from-him-sheikh-ahmad/.

26. "I Hold Yunusa Innocent," *Punch*.

27. "I Hold Yunusa Innocent," *Punch*.

28. "I Hold Yunusa Innocent," *Punch*.

29. Elliot Kaufman, "California Imam Blames the Jews . . . For ISIS,"
National Review, August 25, 2017, https://www.nationalreview
.com/corner/imam-isis-created-israel/.

30. George Washington, letter to Moses Seixas, August 17, 1790,
quoted in "Today in History–August 17," Library of Congress,
accessed June 30, 2020, https://www.loc.gov/item/today-in
-history/august-17/#to-bigotry-no-sanction-to-persecution
-no-assistance.

31. Cardinal Timothy Dolan, "Please Don't Forget Us," Timothy
Cardinal Dolan (blog), January 30, 2015, http://cardinaldolan
.org/index.php/please-dont-forget-us/.

32. Alexander Smith, "Boko Haram Torches Nigerian Town of Baga;
2,000 Missing: Senator," NBC News, January 8, 2015, https://
www.nbcnews.com/storyline/missing-nigeria-schoolgirls
/boko-haram-torches-nigerian-town-baga-2-000-missing
-senator-n282291.

33. Dolan, "Please Don't Forget Us."

34. Dolan, "Please Don't Forget Us."

Chapter 8: The Moral Imperative to Act

1. Authors' direct translation from the Hebrew text.

2. Hila Ratzabi, "Who Was Rabbi Akiva?," My Jewish Learning, accessed May 24, 2020, https://www.myjewishlearning.com /article/rabbi-akiba/.

3. Mishnah Nedarim 9:4 (also in Sifra on Levitcus 19:18), quoted in Barry W. Holtz, *Rabbi Akiva: Sage of the Talmud* (New Haven, CT: Yale University Press, 2017), 174.

4. Holtz, *Rabbi Akiva*, 175.

5. This is the translation of Genesis 5:1 as presented in the Torah.

6. Authors' direct translation of Leviticus 19:16 from the Hebrew text.

7. Authors' direct translation from the Hebrew text.

8. Maimonides, Book of Mitzvot, Prohibitions 207.

9. "Martin Niemöller: 'First They Came for the Socialists,'" United States Holocaust Memorial Museum, last modified March 30, 2012, https://encyclopedia.ushmm.org/content/en/article /martin-niemoeller-first-they-came-for-the-socialists.

10. This and all other Simon Wiesenthal quotes that are not cited are as coauthor Rabbi Abraham Cooper remembers hearing them in the presence of his colleague of thirty years and in personal conversations with him. Rabbi Cooper's only intent is to convey to readers the teachings of this great man and carry on the legacy of Simon Wiesenthal.

11. Rabbi Marvin Hier, "A Tribute to Simon Wiesenthal in His 95th Year," Museum of Tolerance, 2003, http://www .museumoftolerance.com/about-us/about-simon-wiesenthal /a-tribute-to-simon-wiesenthal-in-his-95th-year.html.

12. Hier, "Tribute to Simon Wiesenthal."

13. Hier, "Tribute to Simon Wiesenthal."

14. Hier, "Tribute to Simon Wiesenthal."

15. Rabbi Tarfon, *Ethics of the Fathers* 2:16, Jewish Virtual Library, accessed July 27, 2020, https://www.jewishvirtuallibrary.org /ethics-of-the-fathers-pirkei-avot.

Chapter 9: What Can Be Done to Help

1. Authors' paraphrase of the Hebrew text.

2. "Special Report: 620 Nigerian Christians Hacked to Death in 4 Months—Intersociety," News Express, May 15, 2020, https://newsexpressngr.com/news/98078.

3. "620 Nigerian Christians Hacked to Death," News Express.

4. Michael Dorstewitz, "Faith Leaders Warn Nigeria a 'Ticking Time Bomb' for Christians," Newsmax, February 27, 2020, https://www.newsmax.com/michaeldorstewitz/faith-leaders-christians-nigeria/2020/02/27/id/956008/.

5. "Shekau Weeps in New Audio Over Onslaught by Nigerian Troops + Audio," Eagle Online, May 12, 2020, https://theeagleonline.com.ng/shekau-weeps-in-new-audio-over-onslaught-by-nigerian-troops/.

6. M. O. M. Akpor-Robaro and F. O. Lanre-Babalola, "Nomadic Fulani Herdsmen Turn Terrorists? Exploring the Situation and the Security Implications for Nigeria," IOSR Journal of Humanities and Social Science 23, no. 7, ver. 4 (2018): 48.

7. Cardinal Donald Wuerl, "Cardinal Wuerl's Remarks," Basilica of the National Shrine of the Immaculate Conception, August 28, 2014, transcript, Catholic University of America, https://communications.cua.edu/news/2014/08/wuerl-holy-spirit-remarks.html.

8. Ann Buwalda, quoted in Samuel Smith, "Fulani Killings of Nigerian Christians Meets Standard for 'Genocide,' Jubilee Campaign Says," Christian Post, July 22, 2019, https://www.christianpost.com/news/fulani-killings-of-nigerian-christians-meets-standard-for-genocide-jubilee-campaign-says.html.

ABOUT THE AUTHORS

Rev. Johnnie Moore is a noted speaker, author, and human rights activist. He serves as the president of Congress of Christian Leaders and is the founder of The Kairos Company, one of America's leading boutique communications consultancies. Moore is best known for his extensive multifaith work at the intersection of faith and foreign policy throughout the world but especially in the Middle East.

Moore has been named one of America's twenty-five most influential evangelicals, and he is the youngest recipient of the Simon Wiesenthal Center's prestigious medal of valor for his extensive work on behalf of threatened Christians in the Middle East, an honor he shared with the late Israeli prime minister Shimon Peres (posthumously) that same evening.

Moore serves as a presidential appointee to the United States Commission on International Religious Freedom and sits on many boards, including those of World Help and the National Association of Evangelicals. He also serves on the Anti-Defamation League's Middle East Task Force and is on the advisory board of the ADL-Aspen Institute's Civil Society Fellowship. He is a fellow at the Townsend Institute for Leadership and Counseling at Concordia University Irvine. His undergraduate and graduate studies were in religion at Liberty University.

Rabbi Abraham Cooper is associate dean and director of the Global Social Action Agenda of the Simon Wiesenthal Center, a leading Jewish human rights organization with more than four hundred thousand member families.

In 1977, Rabbi Cooper came to Los Angeles to help Rabbi Marvin Hier found the Simon Wiesenthal Center, giving him the remarkable privilege to know and work with Simon Wiesenthal, of blessed memory, for nearly thirty years. A noted expert on hate on the Internet, Rabbi Cooper has testified before the UN, US Congress, French Parliament, and Japanese Diet. His multifaith activities extend from Azerbaijan to Indonesia, and from India to Japan to Sudan to Kurdistan. He is also a founding member of Israel's Global Forum on Antisemitism.

Rabbi Cooper has a BA and MS from Yeshiva University and a PhD from the Jewish University of America. *Newsweek* has listed Rabbi Cooper, together with Rabbi Hier, as number eight among America's top fifty rabbis.

In 2020, Reverend Moore and Rabbi Cooper were together named among America's ten most influential religious leaders by *Newsmax*. Each travels the world, annually meeting with heads of state, influential religious figures, and leaders in civil society to promote human rights and religious freedom.

SIMON
WIESENTHAL
CENTER

Leadership with
a global reach.

THE
KAIROS
COMPANY

INFLUENCING MILLIONS.

STRATEGY
PUBLIC RELATIONS
COMMUNICATIONS
ADVERTISING

OFFICE@THEKCOMPANY.CO

The Persecution Fund

TO ASSIST IN ADVOCACY FOR THE PERSECUTED
AND PROVIDE PRACTICAL HELP IN THEIR
TIME OF NEED, DONATE TO:

WWW.PERSECUTIONFUND.COM

The
Congress of
Christian Leaders